Traditional Quebec Cooking

A treasure of heirloom recipes

Micheline-Mongrain-Dontigny

Published by:

LES EDITIONS LA BONNE RECETTE

Reprinted: 1997, 2000, 2004

Canadian Cataloguing in publication Data

Mongrain Dontigny, Micheline, 1950-

Traditional Quebec cooking : a treasure of heirloom recipes

Includes index.

ISBN 2-9804058-2-5

1. Cookery, French-Canadian - Quebec style. I. Title.

TX715.6.M673 1995 641.59714 C95-940810-X

Cover design by Sébastien Dontigny

Food pictures by François Croteau

Other pictures by the author

Interior design by Daniel Dontigny

Published by:

Les Editions La bonne Recette

www3.sympatico.ca/edition.bonnerecette/

Printed and bound in Canada

To my dear friend Mireille Lauzon-Dauth who has always believed in my work.

Acknowledgment

I wish to thank Mr. Donald Todd who has revised all the texts in this cookbook. Merci beaucoup!

RELEVE DE TRANSACTION/TRANSACTION RECORD

TPV00000852 MARCH86253202 MC00862532
     LIBRAIRIE PANTOUTE
     1100 RUE ST JEAN
     QUEBEC   QC
Carte/Card:Mastercard
No. 5491 23** **** 5618 07/08
Seq.: 0030 Lot/Batch: 408
2007/07/02 19:15 D@1
     ACHAT/PURCHASE   17.97 $
AUTOR./AUTHOR.: 002618

x _Janet R Anderson_
                JANET R ANDERSON

     00 APPROUVEE - MERCI

Table of Contents

INTRODUCTION 11

HISTORY 13

HORS D'OEUVRES .15
    Potted Pork 16
    Microwaved Potted Pork 17
    Marinated Broad Beans 18
    Grilled Slices of Salted Pork 19
    Roast Dripping Jelly 20

SOUPS 21
    Cabbage Soup 22
    Broad Beans Soup 23
    Drunkard Soup .24
    Pea Soup 25
    Tomato and Milk Soup 26
    Vegetable Soup .27
    Vegetable and Meatball Soup 28
    Hominy and Vegetable Soup 29
    Cream of Partridge Soup 30
    Carrot Soup 32

CEREALS AND BEANS 33
    French Toasts 34
    Pancakes 35
    Buckwheat Pancakes 36
    Oatmeal Porridge 37
    Baked Beans and Pork 38
    Maple Syrup Baked Beans 39

FISH AND SEAFOOD 40
    Fish Chowder 41
    Fried Smelts 42
    Cod in Tomato Soup 43
    Oven Baked Landlocked Salmon 44
    Landlocked Salmon Tourtière 45

Potato Salmon Pie 46
Salmon Sauce 47
Iles de Sorel Fricassee 48
Fish and Chips 49

PORK 50
Pork Roast and Yellow Potatoes 51
Roast Pork and Roast Dripping Jelly 52
Homemade Sausages 53
Pig's Feet and Meatball Ragout 54
Maple Pork Chops 56
Fricassed Sausages 57
Deep Dish Meat Pie 58
Meatpie 60
Ham Croquettes 62
Blood Pudding in White Sauce 63
Salted Pork .64

BEEF AND VEAL 65
Braised Beef with Browned Potatoes 66
Meatballs and Vegetable Stew 67
Boiled Beef and Vegetables 68
Beef Fricassee 69
Mummy's Tomato Meatloaf 70
Quebec Sheperd's Pie 71
Beef Roll 72
Meatballs in Chicken Broth 74
Veal and Pork Patties 75

POULTRY 76
Boiled Chicken and Vegetables 77
Roast Chicken and Meatballs 78
Chicken au Gratin 80

GAME 81
Moose Roast .82
Creamed Partridge 83
Cognac Flambé Partridge 84
Beans and Partridges 85
Partridge with Cabbage 86
Braised Pheasant 87
Saguenay Meat and Game Pie 87

EGGS 88
   Salted Pork Omelette 89
   Eggs in a White Onion Sauce 90
   Pickled Eggs 91

VEGETABLES 92
   Mashed Potatoes and Carrots 93
   Roast Potatoes .94
   Sauteed Cabbage and Onions 94

DESSERTS 95
   Butter Cake 96
   Buttercake with Penuche Sauce 97
   Caramel Cake .98
   Buttercake with Lemon Sauce 100
   Molasses Cake .101
   Yule Log 102
   Small Chocolate Cream Filled Cakes 104
   Poor Man's Pudding 106
   Maple Syrup Pudding 107
   Chocolate Pudding 108
   Strawberry Pudding 109
   Blueberry Pudding 110
   Apple Pudding .111
   Apple Crisp 112
   Rhubarb Crisp .113
   Dumplings in Maple Syrup 114
   Blueberry Dumplings 115
   Grandmother's White Soft Cookies 116
   Molasses Soft Cookies 117
   Syrup Soft Cookies 118
   Chocolate Soft Cookies 119
   Pumpkin Soft Cookies 120
   Blueberry Soft Cookies 121
   Doughnuts 122
   Sugar Pie 123
   Molasses Pie 124
   Apple Pie 124
   Blueberry Pie 126
   Mom's Raisin Pie 127
   Deep Dish Blueberry Pie 128
   Apple Sauce 129

Apple Mousse 130
Maple Sugar Treat 131
Pie Dough 132

CANDIES 133
Penuche 134
St.Catherine Taffy 135
Sponge Taffy 136

PRESERVES 137
Red Tomato ketchup 138
Green Tomato Ketchup 139
Pickled Beets 140
Cucumber Relish 141
Winter Salad 142
Salted Herbs 143
Raspberry Jam .144
Strawberry Jam 145

MENUS 146

INDEX 153

INTRODUCTION

The idea of writing this book came to me a few years ago when I became interested in foreign cuisine. I particularly like foreign cookbooks because they allow me to discover the culture of different countries and regions, and to taste delicious culinary specialties. With this collection of recipes, I want to have you taste the culinary treasures of Quebec and have you learn about the traditional foods of the Quebec people.

As a young newlywed, I quickly realized that our traditional cooking was not limited only to my mother's and my grandmother's familiar dishes. I soon discovered, in my husband's family and in those of friends, other Quebec culinary treasures which I eagerly wrote in my notebook of recipes. It was only the beginning of an index of Québécois recipes which were going to later allow me to write this book. Since many dishes were prepared without a recipe, I didn't hesitate to go and learn how to prepare them. The collected information was often passed on to me by word of mouth while I watched the cook who was preparing the dish. My mother-in-law is the first person who was willing to share her precious time to teach me how to prepare tasty dishes such as "ragoût de pattes" (pig's feet), "le saumon en sauce blanche" (salmon in white sauce) and "la galette de sarrasin" (buckwheat pancakes).

The Cuisine of Quebec is a simple cuisine prepared with few ingredients. Since the women had to share in the many tasks on the farm, most meals were prepared in very little time. They let a soup or stew simmer on the stove for many hours. The utensils and stew pot were made of cast iron and this gave a characteristic flavor to the dishes. Pork and beans and braised meat cooked in a cast iron cauldron don't have the same taste as when they are cooked in a cauldron which is not made of cast iron.

The Cuisine of Quebec is based mainly on the cultures of the American Indian, the French and the English. Corn, beans and wild meat came from the Indians, pastry such as pies and tartes, and soups originated from the French while the fried fish dishes, puddings and oatmeal are from the influence of the English.

One finds the same dishes all over the province with the exception of some specialties which characterize each of the regions. Fish and seafood often appear on menus in Gaspé and on the North Shore; the wild meat dishes are popular in Mauricie and the Saguenay-Lac-St-Jean. The Beauce region, the largest producer of maple sap products in Quebec and in North America, make much use of maple syrup. The most popular cheese, dear to the Quebec people, is fresh cheddar cheese, especially the curd. They make it everywhere in the province and, travellers as well as the local people can obtain some from different cheese factories and have the opportunity to savor the fresh rounds of cheese of the day. With the growing interest by the Quebec people for other types of cheese one now finds that a greater variety of cheeses are made in Quebec. We should not forget the Oka cheese, which is made in Oka, and whose reputation is second to none. This cheese is known everywhere in the world.

The Québécois really like to entertain. Instead of sending formal invitations, they share their meals with family and friends who just drop in. If they are invited, it is often on the spur of the moment...

HISTORY

The first people to arrive in Quebec were explorers who were sent by the King of France. The King wanted to discover and conquer a new land in order to increase his power throughout the world. The explorers discovered a land rich in furbearing animals that could easily be trapped and converted into furs for the rich and well-to-do people of France. The first people to make a living in Quebec were hunters and trappers "coureurs des bois"; their job was to travel to all parts of Quebec to trade with the Indians.

A little later, the King of France wanted Quebec to become more prosperous and eventually dominate North America. Since the colony consisted mostly of men, the King sent boatloads full of women to Quebec to marry and raise families which would help to assure the prosperity of the colony. These women were called "Les Filles du Roy". There is today, a restaurant in Montreal, that has this name and which serves typical Québécois meals.

The first colonists had to adapt to other ways of providing for food for themselves despite the fact that they had brought provisions from their homeland. As the days passed by, they had to learn from the Indians how to survive the rigorous winter climate. The Indians showed them how to hunt and taught them about the fruits and vegetables that could be gathered from the forest. Certain explorers' records indicate that some people died of hunger because they did not want to eat food that they were not familiar with.

Through the years the inhabitants started to grow vegetables and to raise livestock to supply the needs of the family. The meals were prepared in the same way as was done in their mother country, France. They used other ingredients when the original ones were not available. Certain traditional Quebec dishes, such as "soupe aux pois" (pea soup) is still very popular throughout Quebec, and can be traced back to the old French cookbooks.

After several wars between France and England, the capture

of Quebec City by the English brought the fighting to an end in 1759 and Quebec was henceforth governed by England. Even though France had lost the war, the Quebec people were allowed to speak their own language, to practice their religion and to keep their traditions. Inevitably, with two nations living side by side, the ingredients used by the English in their cooking contributed to enrich the traditional Quebec cuisine.

Nowadays, the Quebec people remain very attached to their traditional cooking and are very proud of it, even though they have integrated much international cuisine into their daily menu.

HORS D'OEUVRES

At one time, there were no such things as hors d'oeuvres included in a French Canadian meal.

The recipes that follow were served as an accompaniment to the meal. Today they are served as hors d'oeuvres or entrées.

CRETONS

Potted Pork

This recipe comes from Mrs Gilberte Morin Martinson. She came to La Tuque with her family, 68 years ago. For maximum flavor, prepare "Cretons" two days before you plan to serve them.

1¹/₂ lb	shoulder of pork	750 g
1	pork kidney, trimmed	1
2	small chopped onions	2
1	clove of garlic	1
	Salt and pepper	
¹/₄ tsp	ground allspice	2 ml
1 cup	boiling water	250 ml

1. Grind pork and pork kidney, in meat grinder. Mince garlic.
2. Place meat mixture, onions, garlic, water and seasonings in a casserole. Add boiling water - water level should come to ³/₄ of level of meat mixture - add water as needed; add more boiling water if necessary.
3. Stir well with a wooden spoon, bring to a boil and simmer for 2 hours.
4. Adjust seasoning to taste.
5. Pour mixture into small bowls which have been rinsed under cold water. Cool to room temperature.
6. Place in refrigerator to cool completely. Potted pork is ready when mixture is firm to the touch.
7. To serve, place a slice of potted pork on a leaf of lettuce and garnish with pickles and a piece of tomato. Accompany with bread.

> Potted pork will keep for four days in the refrigerator and two months in the freezer.

CRETONS AU MICRO-ONDES
Microwaved Potted Pork

This is a lean version of potted pork.

1 lb	ground pork	454 g
1	medium onion, chopped	1
12	soda crackers	12
1	garlic clove minced	1
1 cup	milk	250 ml
	Salt and pepper	
	A pinch of ground cinnamon	
	A pinch of ground cloves	

1. Place all ingredients into a microwave casserole. Mix well.
2. Microwave on High for 15 minutes stirring every 5 minutes.
3. For a smoother texture, blend the mixture in a food processor for a few seconds. Cool to room temperature and place in the refrigerator until set, at least 2 hours.

GOURGANES À LA VINAIGRETTE
Marinated Broad Beans

1 cup	fresh or frozen broad beans	250 ml
1 tbsp	vinegar	15 ml
1/4 tsp	paprika	1 ml
1/4 cup	vegetable oil	60 ml
1/2 tsp	worcestershire sauce	2 ml
	Salt and pepper	

1. Boil the broad beans in a large pot of salted water until tender but still firm.
2. Rinse in cold water and peel outer skin.
3. In a small bowl, mix together the vinegar, paprika, vegetable oil, worcestershire sauce, salt and pepper.
4. Place the peeled broad beans in the dressing and marinate for at least one hour.
5. To serve, place a leaf of lettuce on a small plate, spoon the marinated beans into the lettuce and garnish with a piece of tomato and a sprig of parsley.

SERVES *4*

GRILLADES DE LARD
Grilled Slices of Salted Pork

Sometimes these are called "oreilles de crisse". This expression probably originates from the word "ear" since the slices of salted pork curl up and look like big ears during the cooking.

1	*piece of salted pork (half meat, half fat)*	1

1. Slice the salted pork $1/8$ inch thick.
2. Place the slices into a small pot, cover with cold water and bring to a boil.
3. Remove the slices of salted pork from the water and rinse in cold water to cool.
4. Brown the slices on both sides in a cast iron pan. Set the heat on low until some melted fat appears; continue the cooking on medium heat and stir occasionally. The slices of salted pork should have a crisp texture when ready.
5. These slices may accompany the meal or may be served as hors d'oeuvres.

Roast Dripping Jelly

To prepare roast dripping jelly see roast pork and roast dripping jelly.

Serve with bread and pickles.

SOUPS

Soups were very important in the early days of Quebec. At an early age, grandma's kitchen was the place where I first tasted so many delicious Quebec dishes. Her memorable soups with their "homey" aroma were prepared daily with the same broth but using different ingredients for variation.

They were nutritious and inexpensive to feed a large family.

SOUPE AU CHOU
Cabbage Soup

$^1/_2$ lb	green cabbage thinly sliced	250 g
2 oz	salted pork	60 g
1	medium onion chopped	1
1	medium tomato peeled and chopped	1
5 cups	beef broth	1,25 litre
1	garlic clove minced	1
	Salt and pepper	

1. Cut the salted pork into small cubes. Sauté in a casserole until browned.
2. Add onions and cook on medium heat until they become translucent.
3. Add cabbage, broth and seasonings; simmer for $1^1/_2$ hours.
4. Add the chopped tomato 15 minutes before the end of cooking.

SERVES 6

SOUPE AUX GOURGANES
Broad Beans Soup

"Soupe aux gourganes" originates from the Saguenay Lac St-Jean region. While travelling in this area, you will notice that some restaurants advertise their regional dishes such as "Soupe aux gourganes", "Tarte aux bleuets" and "Tourtière du Saguenay". This soup can be served for a light lunch accompanied with fresh bread and cheese.

³/₄ lb	salted pork	350 g
1¹/₂ lb	beef shank	680 g
¹/₂ cup	barley	125 ml
1	large onion chopped	1
2 cups	fresh or frozen broad beans	500 ml
¹/₂ cup	wax beans chopped	125 ml
12	small carrots	12
2	sticks of celery with leaves on, chopped	2
1 cup	fresh herbs, chopped (chives, green onions, parsley)	250 ml
6	new potatoes diced (optional)	6

1. Place the salted pork, the beef, the barley and onion into a large pot; add 3 quarts (3 liters) of water and bring to a boil.
2. Add the broad beans and the wax beans and simmer for 3 hours.
3. Add the carrots, celery, and fresh herbs ¹/₂ hour before the end of cooking. If using potatoes, add them with the vegetables.
4. When the vegetables are cooked, remove the salted pork and beef shank from the pot. Remove the bones and gristle from the beef and put the meat back into the soup.
5. Season with salt and pepper.
6. This soup can be frozen; if you do so, omit the potatoes.

SERVES 8 TO 12

SOUPE À L'IVROGNE
Drunkard Soup

I was told that in the old days, this soup was very popular for the "day after".

¹/₄ lb	salted pork	125 g
3	large onions chopped	3
6	slices of bread, diced	6
2 quarts	beef broth	2 litres
2 tbsp	salted herbs	30 ml
	Pepper	

1. Rinse the salted herbs in cold water to remove the salt.
2. Cut the salted pork in dices and brown in a saucepan.
3. Add the bread and cook at 350°F (175°C) for 10 minutes. Remove from oven.
4. Add the broth and salted herbs and simmer for one hour.
5. Season with pepper.

SERVES 10

SOUPE AUX POIS
Pea Soup

Pea soup is usually served during the winter months since there are fewer fresh vegetables available. It's also very comforting.

$^1/_2$ lb	salted pork (or one ham bone)	225 g
1 lb	yellow peas	454 g
1	large onion, chopped	1
$^1/_2$ cup	chopped celery with leaves	125 ml
$^1/_4$ cup	fresh parsley	60 ml
1	bay leaf	1
1 tsp	dried savory	5 ml
	Salt	
10 cups	cold water	2,5 litres

1. Wash peas and soak overnight in cold water.
2. Rinse peas and pour into a large pot.
3. Add water and the rest of the ingredients to the peas, bring to a boil, cover and simmer for 3 hours until the peas become very soft.
4. Remove salted pork or ham bone. For a creamier consistency, purée half of the soup in a blender or a food processor. Return the purée into the soup and season to taste.
5. This soup can be frozen for 6 months.

SERVES 8

SOUPE AUX TOMATES ET AU LAIT

Tomato and Milk Soup

1	medium onion chopped	1
5	fresh or canned tomatoes cut in chunks	5
1 tsp	sugar	5 ml
1¹/₂ tbsp	butter	20 ml
¹/₈ tsp	baking soda	0,5 ml
2 cups	milk	500 ml
	Salt and pepper	

1. Melt the butter in a pan, the butter should not brown. Add onions and cook on low heat for 5 minutes. Add the sugar and tomatoes. Remove from heat.
2. Add the baking soda and stir well until there is no more scum.
3. Put back on heat and add the milk. Heat slowly until the milk gets hot; it should not boil.
4. Season with salt and pepper.

SERVES 4

SOUPE AUX LÉGUMES
Vegetable Soup

$^1/_2$ cup	butter	125 ml
$^1/_2$ lb	ground beef	225 g
3	chopped onions	3
3	sticks chopped celery	3
3	chopped carrots	3
1	16 oz (500 ml) can of tomatoes	1
6 cups	water	1,5 litres
	Parsley, chives	
	Salt and pepper	

1. In a medium size pan, sauté the onion in melted butter.
2. Add ground beef, tomatoes, carrots, celery and chives.
3. Bring to a boil, lower the heat and simmer for $1^1/_2$ hours.
4. Season with salt and pepper and garnish with parsley.
5. You can freeze this soup.

SERVES 8

SOUPE AUX LÉGUMES ET BOULETTES
Vegetable and Meatball Soup

6 cups	beef or chicken broth	1,5 litres
2	large tomatoes, canned	2
2	chopped carrots	2
1/2 lb	ground beef	225 g
2 tbsp	salted herbs rinsed in cold water to remove excess salt	30 ml
1/2 cup	fine egg noodles	125 ml
	Pepper	

1. In a medium size pan, simmer the broth, tomatoes, carrots and salted herbs for about 30 minutes.
2. Shape ground beef into tiny sized meatballs; add to the soup with the noodles and simmer 20 minutes.
3. Season with pepper and salt if necessary.

SERVES 8

SOUPE AUX LÉGUMES ET BLÉ D'INDE LESSIVÉ
Hominy and Vegetable Soup

This recipe is one version of my grandmother's soups. She would prepare a big kettle of beef broth at the beginning of the week, which became the base for a different soup for each day of the week. In one version, she added noodles to the broth, in another one, she added one canned chopped tomatoes with salted herbs. Her "Soupe aux légumes et blé d'inde lessivé" is one of my favorites.

6 cups	beef broth	1,5 litres
1	chopped carrot	1
1	chopped celery stalk	1
1 tbsp	salted herbs	15 ml
1 cup	hominy rinsed in cold water	250 ml
	Pepper	

1. In a medium pot, bring the beef broth to a boil.
2. Add the carrot, celery, rinse salted herbs and simmer for one hour.
3. Add hominy, heat for a few minutes, season with pepper and salt if necessary.

SERVES 6

CRÈME DE PERDRIX
Cream of Partridge Soup

I usually prepare this soup when I have leftover partridge carcasses. See "Creamed Partridge" in the game chapter. It is a delicious way to extend the use of these small birds. Carcasses will keep for two days in the refrigerator before you prepare the soup. I don't use the legs of partridges because it gives an undesirable strong taste to the soup.

	Carcasses from 2 partridges without the legs	
2	small onions	2
1	stalk of celery including leaves	1
1	bay leaf	1
	Few whole peppercorns	
	A pinch of thyme, a sprig of parsley	
4 tbsp	butter	60 ml
4 tbsp	flour	60 ml
1¹/₂ cups	milk	375 ml
	Salt and pepper	
	A pinch of instant dry chicken bouillon powder as needed	

1. Place the carcasses of partridge into a medium pot and cover with cold water.
2. Bring to a boil, add one onion, celery stalk, bay leaf, peppercorns, thyme and parsley. Simmer one hour.
3. When the partridge broth is ready, melt the butter in another pan, add the second onion, chopped, and cook on low heat until the onion becomes soft and transparent; add flour and simmer one minute.
4. Add the milk and 1¹/₂ cups of partridge broth, stir well. Bring

to a boil and simmer until the cream thickens.
5. Remove the meat from the cooked carcasses, chop and add
    to the cream. After the chopped meat has been added, do not
    let the soup boil, otherwise the meat will become tough.
6. Season with salt and pepper and serve.

SERVES 4

POTAGE AUX CAROTTES

Carrot Soup

4	large thinly sliced carrots	4
1	medium chopped onion	1
2 tbsp	butter	30 ml
5 cups	beef broth	1 litre
	Salt and pepper	

1. In a medium size pot, melt the butter.
2. On low heat, sauté the carrots and onions in butter for 10 minutes.
3. Add the beef broth, bring to a boil and simmer for 15 minutes.
4. Purée the soup in a blender or a food processor.
5. Season and serve. This soup can be frozen.

SERVES 6

Pea Soup (p. 25)

Typical Gaspesian house

CEREALS AND BEANS

Most of the dishes included in this chapter were served for breakfast. In early times, Québécois worked hard as farmers, lumberjacks and trappers.

Through the years, people changed their lifestyle and eating habits. They now eat lighter breakfasts. I would suggest that you prepare such a breakfast on weekends when you anticipate outdoor activities.

French Toasts

2	eggs	2
4	slices of bread	4
	Granulated white sugar	
	Ground cinnamon	
2 tbsp	vegetable oil	30 ml
2 tbsp	butter	30 ml
	Maple syrup or jam	

1. In a large bottomed bowl, beat the eggs until no more egg white appears in the mixture.
2. Cut slices of bread in diagonals.
3. In a skillet, heat the oil and butter.
4. When the fat in the skillet is very hot, soak the bread in eggs, lift the slice of bread to remove excess eggs and fry in the skillet on both sides. The bread is ready when golden brown.
5. Repeat step 4 for the remaining slices of bread.
6. Remove excess fat from the fried bread with paper towel.
7. Place the fried bread on a cookie sheet, sprinkle with white sugar and cinnamon. Broil the bread for a few seconds until the sugar starts to melt. Serve with maple syrup.

SERVES 2

CRÊPES
Pancakes

Traditionnaly these pancakes were cooked in lard or shortening. Now that we are conscious of fat intake, I suggest the use of vegetable oil as is done in this recipe.

1 cup	all purpose flour	250 ml
2	eggs	2
1 cup	milk	250 ml
1 tbsp	melted butter	15 ml
	A pinch of salt	
1/4 tsp	baking soda	1 ml
	Vegetable oil for cooking	

1. Mix flour, salt and sugar in a bowl.
2. Add milk and eggs and then beat with an electric mixer for one minute or until there are no more lumps. Add butter and baking soda; mix well.
3. On medium high, heat a cast iron skillet. Cover the bottom of the skillet with oil. When the oil is hot pour in just enough pancake mixture to cover the bottom of the skillet.
4. Cook the pancake until the edge lifts away from the skillet. Turn the pancake over and cook for about 30 seconds. You will see brown spots when pancake is lifted.

Pancake batter can be prepared in a mixer or a food processor. Pancakes will keep in the refrigerator for 4 days. Place a piece of wax paper between each pancake; wrap the pancakes in plastic wrap. You can also freeze the pancakes;to defrost, remove the pack of pancakes from the freezer, let thaw for about 15 minutes and remove the number of pancakes needed. Return remaining pancakes to the freezer.

Buckwheat Pancakes

3 cups	buckwheat flour	675 ml
1 tsp	baking soda	5 ml
3/4 tsp	salt	3 ml
4 cups	cold water	1 litre
	Butter, molasses, maple sugar	

1. In a large bowl, mix buckwheat flour, baking soda and salt.
2. Gradually add the cold water, whisk the batter until it has the consistency of thick cream; if necessary add more water.
3. You can cook the pancake directly on a wood stove or on a cast iron stove plate, placed on your electric stove, or else in a cast iron skillet.
4. Heat the utensil used on medium high heat, pour in a small ladle of batter and spread the batter with the back of the ladle. Cook the pancake until it looses its shiny look on the top. Turn over and cook until the pancake becomes a pale golden color underneath.
5. Spread the pancake with butter, molasses or maple sugar and a spoonful of cream; roll it up before eating. Butter, molasses, maple sugar and cream are placed on the table so that each guest can spread the pancakes with his favorite flavor.

SERVES 6

Oatmeal Porridge

1¹/₂ cups	water	350 ml
²/₃ cup	quick cooking oatmeal	175 ml
¹/₄ tsp	salt	2 ml
	Brown sugar	
	Milk or cream	

1. In a medium casserole, bring the water and salt to boil.
2. Add oatmeal, stir and cook on medium heat for 3 minutes.
3. Remove from heat and let rest for a few minutes before serving.
4. Sprinkle each portion with brown sugar and 2 tbsp of milk or cream; mix well.
5. Serve with buttered toast.

In the microwave

1. Combine water, oatmeal and salt in a one quart glass bowl.
2. Microwave on High for 2 minutes, stir and microwave on high for 1 or 2 minutes or until the liquid is absorbed.
3. Let stand for 1 or 2 minutes.
4. Follow step 4 and 5 above.

SERVES 4

Baked Beans and Pork

Beans and pork will have more flavor if baked in a cast iron pot; earthenware dishes are also a good choice to bake beans.

2 cups	white dried pinto beans	500 ml
6 cups	water	1,5 litres
¹/₂ lb	salted pork	225 g
3 tbsp	brown sugar	45 ml
3 tbsp	molasses	45 ml
1 tsp	salt	5 ml
1 tsp	ground dry mustard	5 ml
1 tbsp	ketchup	15 ml
1	medium onion, chopped	1
3 cups	water (approximately)	750 ml

1. Wash beans under cold running water. Soak the beans in 6 cups (1,5 litres) water for 6 to 8 hours; this can be done overnight. Rinse well.
2. Place the beans in a pan, cover with water and boil 10 minutes. Drain in a colander.
3. Place the beans in a large cast iron or earthenware pot, add salted pork, cut in pieces or left whole, brown sugar, molasses, salt, mustard, ketchup, onion and 3 cups (750 ml) water. Cook covered in the oven for about 6 hours at 250°F (140°C).

> This dish can be frozen. If more liquid is needed, add cold water to cold beans or hot water to hot beans.

SERVES 6

FÈVES AU LARD AU SIROP D'ÉRABLE
Maple Syrup Baked Beans

This is a sweeter version of baked beans for those who like maple flavored dishes.

2 cups	dried white beans	500 ml
1¹/₂ quarts	water	1,5 litres
1 tsp	salt	5 ml
¹/₄ lb	salted pork	125 g
¹/₂ cup	maple syrup	125 ml
2 cups	cooking liquid from beans	500 ml
	A pinch of thyme	
	A pinch of pepper	
¹/₂ tsp	dry mustard	2 ml
¹/₂ cup	chopped onion	125 ml
¹/₂ cup	maple syrup	125 ml

1. Soak the dry beans in water overnight.
2. Drain the beans and rinse well in cold water.
3. Place the beans in a medium casserole, add 1¹/₂ quarts of water and salt. Bring to boil, cover and cook on medium for 30 minutes.
4. Drain the beans and save the cooking liquid.
5. Place the beans and salted pork in a bean pot or a cast iron casserole.
6. Mix 2 cups (500 ml) of reserve cooking liquid, ¹/₂ cup (125 ml) maple syrup, thyme, mustard and onion. Pour on top of beans, cover and cook for 6 hours at 250°F (140°C).
7. Uncover, add the other ¹/₂ cup (125 ml) maple syrup and cook for 30 minutes.

SERVES 6

FISH AND SEAFOOD

Most traditional Quebec fish dishes come from areas near the St Lawrence River. In those regions, many people earned their living as fishermen. In other parts of Quebec, the fish were caught in lakes and rivers. In my childhood, fish and seafood were served mostly on abstinence days imposed by the Catholic religion. Since then, the Catholic church has abolished abstinence. There aren't many traditional seafood recipes in Quebec cuisine, but Québécois today love seafood.

There are delicious lobsters and mussels in les Iles-de-la-Madeleine area, succulent small shrimps in Matane and Côte-Nord. In the latter area you can also find queen crabs. It has also been said that people enjoyed eating oysters in the early days of Quebec.

I haven't included seafood recipes in this chapter since seafood dishes prepared by Québécois, are similar to many found in the average cookbooks.

CHAUDRÉE DE POISSON
Fish Chowder

Fish chowder originates from New England. The recipe was brought by the "Empire Loyalists" who settled in Quebec after the American War of Independence. I usually serve fish chowder with bread for lunch.

2 cups	white fish fillets in cubes	500 ml
2 cups	water	500 ml
3 tbsp	butter	45 ml
1 cup	finely chopped celery	250 ml
2 cups	potatoes	500 ml
2 cups	milk	500 ml
1	medium onion, chopped	1
	Salt and pepper to taste	

1. Cut potatoes in small cubes.
2. In a medium casserole, saute onions in butter, add potatoes and celery. Season with salt and pepper.
3. Add water, bring to a boil, cover and simmer until potatoes are half cooked, about 10 minutes.
4. Add fish cubes and simmer for 10 minutes or until fish flakes easily.
5. When vegetables and fish are cooked, add milk. Watch milk while heating, it should not boil. Check seasoning.
6. Fish chowder isn't very good when reheated; prepare only the amount needed.

SERVES 4

Fried Smelts

You can serve these small fried fish as an entrée. Place about five per serving on a bed of lettuce. Serve with tartar sauce and a lemon wedge.

¹/₂ lb	*smelts*	*225 g*
	Salt and pepper	
1	*egg*	*1*
2 tbsp	*water*	*30 ml*
	Dash of vegetable oil	
³/₄ cup	*flour*	*175 ml*
³/₄ cup	*dry breadcrumbs*	*175 ml*
	Vegetable oil for frying	

1. Gut the smelts if necessary. Cut off heads, tails and fins. Wash under cold running water.
2. In a bowl, mix egg, water, oil, salt and pepper.
3. Dip smelts in flour, shake off excess flour. Dip in egg mixture. Dip in breadcrumbs and press firmly on fish; shake off to remove excess breadcrumbs.
4. Heat 3 inches of oil in a deep casserole at 360°F (180°C). Fry the smelts a few at a time until golden brown. Place fried fishes on paper towel to remove excess oil. Serve immediately or keep in a warm oven no longer than half an hour.

SERVES *2*

MORUE À LA SOUPE AUX TOMATES
Cod in Tomato Soup

Fresh cod is plentiful in the Gaspésie and Côte-Nord areas. You can substitute cod for any white flesh fish.

1 cup	chopped onions	250 ml
3 tbsp	butter	45 ml
1 tbsp	all purpose flour	15 ml
2 lb	cod fillets	1 kg
	Salt and pepper	
1	10 oz (300 ml) tomato soup can	1
1 cup	water	250 ml

1. Sauté the onions in butter until golden.
2. Add flour and mix well.
3. In an ovenproof casserole, place cod fillets on top of onion mixture.
4. Season with salt and pepper.
5. Mix tomato soup with water; pour on top of fish.
6. Cover and cook at 400°F (200°C) for about 20 minutes or until fish flakes easily.

SERVES 4

OUANANICHE AU FOUR
Oven Baked Landlocked Salmon

"Ouananiche" is a very popular fish caught mainly in the Saguenay-Lac-St-Jean area. The flavor of "ouananiche" is as delicate as salmon.You can substitute salmon or a big lake trout for the "ouananiche" in this recipe. Since "ouananiche" is not caught commercially, it is not possible to buy any at the store.

1	Landlocked Salmon of about 3 lb (1¹/₂ kg)	1
	Foil paper to wrap the fish	
1	medium carrot, finely chopped	1
1	medium onion, finely chopped	1
¹/₂ cup	dry white wine	125 ml
1 tbsp	butter	15 ml
3	lemon slices, zest and peel removed	3
	Salt and pepper	

1. On low heat, sauté carrots and onions in butter until soft and transparent.
2. Cut two sheets of foil, long enough to wrap the fish.
3. Scatter cooked vegetables on foil and lay the fish on top.
4. Season with salt and pepper, cover with lemon slices.
5. Raise the foil on each side of fish to prevent wine from running out. Pour wine on top of fish.
6. Fold the long sides of the foil twice leaving a space between the fish and the foil; fold the narrow ends of the foil twice.
7. Place the package on a cookie sheet and cook at 450°F (230°C) for 10 minutes for each inch (2 cm) of thickness.
8. Serve the fish with cooking broth, baked potatoes and green vegetables.

TOURTIÈRE À LA OUANANICHE
Landlocked Salmon Tourtière

You can substitute salmon for the landlocked salmon in this recipe.

1 lb	landlocked salmon	454 g
1	large potato, thinly sliced	1
1	medium onion, sliced	1
2 tbsp	butter	30 ml
1/4 cup	milk	60 ml
2 tbsp	heavy cream	30 ml
	Salt and pepper	
	Pie dough for two crusts (see index)	

1. Bone the salmon and cut into small pieces.
2. On medium heat, sauté the onions until transparent.
3. In a large bowl, mix all ingredients except the pie dough.
4. Line a large pie plate with pie dough. Pour in the fish mixture and add cold water to half the depth of the fish mixture.
5. Cover with second pie dough, sealing dough with egg wash.
6. Cut a two inch (5 cm) hole in center of pie and brush surface with egg wash.
7. Cook at 350°F (175°C) for 1¹/₂ hours.
8. Serve with green salad and pickles.

SERVES 4

PÂTÉ AU SAUMON
Potato Salmon Pie

This dish was very popular on abstinence days imposed by the Catholic religion.

2 cups	canned salmon	500 ml
3 cups	mashed potatoes	750 ml
1/2 cup	finely chopped onions	125 ml
3 tbsp	butter	45 ml
1/2 tsp	salt	2 ml
1/4 tsp	savory (optional)	1 ml
	Pepper	
	Pie dough for two crusts (see index)	

1. Drain salmon broth from can. Bone and clean salmon; break into small pieces.
2. Sauté onions in butter until transparent; set aside.
3. In medium bowl, mix mashed potatoes, salmon, cooked onions and seasoning. Cool to room temperature.
4. While mixture is cooling, prepare pie dough.
5. Transfer potato salmon mixture to pie shell. Brush edge of dough with egg wash and cover with top crust.
6. Seal edges and brush pie with egg wash. Don't brush edges; it will brown too much during the baking. Cut slits and cook at 400°C (220°C) for about 25 minutes until crust is golden brown.
7. Serve with green salad and pickles.

SERVES 4

SAUCE AU SAUMON
Salmon Sauce

The first time I ate this dish, it was prepared by my mother-in-law. There were unexpected guests, so she took out a can of salmon from her pantry and prepared "Sauce au saumon". I found it was so simple and delicious that I asked her to show me how to prepare it; she didn't have a measured recipe. For a chicken version, she adds chopped green peppers in place of the onions and substitutes the salmon with cooked chicken. Serve with boiled potatoes. For a more modern version, I sometimes add chopped capers to "Sauce au saumon".

4 tbsp	butter	60 ml
4 tbsp	flour	60 ml
1	small onion, chopped	1
2 cups	milk	500 ml
1 lb	salmon can	454 g
	Salt and pepper	

1. Melt butter in a medium casserole. Sauté onions until transparent.
2. Add flour, mix well and cook on low heat until it bubbles.
3. Add milk, mix well with a whisk. Bring to boil, stir and cook on medium heat until thicken.
4. Add salmon, free of skin and bones and then add seasoning.

SERVES 4

GIBELOTTE DES ILES DE SOREL
Iles de Sorel Fricassee

This dish is very popular in the town of Sorel, eastern Quebec. "Gibelotte" is celebrated with festivities each summer in this town. Commonly, perch and catfish are used, but you can substitute any white fish.

2 tbsp	butter	30 ml
2	medium onions, chopped	2
1/4 cup	chopped celery	65 ml
	Salt and pepper	
1/4 tsp	savory	1 ml
1 cup	beef broth	250 ml
4	medium carrots, sliced	4
4	diced potatoes	4
1/2 lb	green beans	225 g
1/2 cup	cream of tomato soup	125 ml
1/2 cup	creamed corn	125 ml
1/2 cup	frozen green peas	125 ml
1 lb	fish fillets (catfish, perch)	454 g

1. In a large casserole, sauté onions and celery in butter.
2. Add beef broth and seasonings.
3. Add carrots, potatoes, beans, cream of tomato soup and simmer until vegetables are almost done.
4. Add creamed corn, peas and fish. Cover and simmer until fish flakes easily.

SERVES *4*

Fish and Chips

"Fish and Chips" is the name given to this dish in Quebec. This is a typical example of English influence on Quebec Cuisine. Serve with French Fries and coleslaw.

1 cup	flour	250 ml
2 tsp	baking powder	10 ml
1¹/₄ tsp	salt	6 ml
1 tsp	sugar	5 ml
1 tbsp	vegetable oil	15 ml
¹/₂ cup	milk	125 ml
¹/₂ cup	water	125 ml
1 lb	sole or haddock fillets	454 g
	Salt and pepper	
	Flour for dipping fish	
	Vegetable oil for deep frying	

1. Mix and sift dry ingredients.
2. Mix together oil, water and milk.
3. Gradually whisk liquid into dry ingredients. Set aside. This can also be done in food processor.
4. Cut fillets into 3 inch (15 cm) pieces, season with salt and pepper.
5. Dip pieces of fish in flour, shake off excess flour and dip in batter and fry in oil until brown. Drain on paper towel to remove excess oil.

SERVES 3 TO 4

PORK

Occasionnally, Quebecers are nicknamed "Mangeurs de soupe aux pois et lard" (pea soup and pork eaters). The reason for this, is that these dishes were their staple diet in the early days of Quebec. One wouldn't think of Quebec Cuisine without pork meat. Pigs were slaughtered in late autumn when the temperature was below freezing. They froze meat outside or in an unheated part of the house. Pieces of meat were cut as needed during the winter months. Pork fat was melted and strained and was used for cooking and pastry.

Cuts of pork were and still are transformed into salt pork, which is extensively used in Quebec Cuisine, smoked ham, sausages, pork pâté and blood puddings. Pork heads are converted into "tête fromagée" (head cheese), a kind of pâté. Nowadays, head cheese is rarely prepared at home; Quebecers buy it at the butcher shop.

RÔTI DE PORC ET PATATES JAUNES
Pork Roast and Yellow Potatoes

This roast, usually served on Sundays, is a favorite. One can serve either beets, green vegetables or a salad with the roast.

3 lb	pork loin roast	1,5 kg
1	piece of pork rind about 3 inches (10 cm) square, fat removed	1
3	cloves of garlic	3
1	medium sliced onion	1
	Salt and pepper	
1 tbsp	dry mustard	15 ml
2 tbsp	soft butter	30 ml
¹/₂ tsp	dry marjoram	3 ml
1 cup	water	250 ml
4 to 6	small peeled potatoes	4 to 6

1. Cut cloves of garlic in two. With a small knife, make six incisions in roast. Push garlic pieces into incisions in meat.
2. Season roast with salt and pepper.
3. In a small bowl, mix together dry mustard and soft butter. Brush lean parts of roast with this mixture.
4. Place pork rind in a 9 x 13 inch roasting pan. Put sliced onion on top of rind. Lay roast on top of onion and sprinkle with marjoram.
5. Pour water into bottom of pan.
6. Cook uncovered for one hour at 350°F (175°C), put peeled potatoes around roast in cooking juice and cook for one hour. Turn over potatoes and cook for another hour. Roast should be basted every 15 minutes or so during those 3 cooking hours.
7. If cooking juice disappears while roasting, you can add a little water. Before serving meat and potatoes with cooking juice, tip the pan and remove melted fat on top of juice.

SERVES 4 TO 6

RÔTI DE LARD ET GRAISSE DE RÔTI
Roast Pork and Roast Dripping Jelly

When preparing this dish you get two dishes in one; a roast and roast dripping jelly. Roast dripping jelly is made with cooking juice obtained while cooking meat. Grandmother says that roast dripping jelly was more favored by men than women in her time. For best result, use a cast iron pot. Explanations on how to serve roast dripping jelly are given in the Appetizers chapter.

3 lb	pork shoulder roast	1,5 kg
2	medium onions cut into chunks	2
1	garlic clove	1
1	piece of pork rind about 3 inches (10 cm) square	1
	Salt and pepper	
1 cup	water	250 ml

1. Cut small fat pieces from roast and melt on low heat in a saucepan.
2. Cut garlic in two pieces and insert in roast.
3. On medium heat, brown roast on all sides in melted fat. This operation will take about 20 minutes. Remove roast from casserole. Brown onions and put roast back into casserole. Add pork rind cut in squares.
4. Cover and cook on low heat for 4 hours. Baste and turn roast once in a while; if it stick to the casserole, add a little water.
5. When cooking is finished, remove roast from casserole, reduce cooking liquid by half, add the water, scrape the bottom of the pan with a spatula and simmer mixture for 10 minutes. Check seasoning, strain and pour cooking juice into small bowls rinsed under cold water.
6. Serve roast with some juice and put leftover juice in refrigerator; that will be your pork dripping jelly.
7. Serve roast with vegetables such as mashed potatoes, carrots or beets.

SERVES 6

SAUCISSES MAISON
Homemade Sausages

This simple recipe comes from the mother of my friend Carmen Boisclair. It's a handy recipe because you don't need sausage casings, which aren't always easy to find. Shape sausages with sausage funnel or use your hands to shape into patties.

10 lb	ground beef	5 kg
5 lb	ground pork	2,5 kg
5 tsp	ground cinnamon	25 ml
$2^1/_2$ tsp	ground clove	12 ml
1 tsp	pepper	5 ml
8 tsp	salt	40 ml
1 cup	all purpose flour	250 ml
$1^1/_2$ cups	water	375 ml

1. Mix all ingredients together.
2. Attach sausage funnel to meat grinder, omitting four armed cutter and round disc.
3. Put meat mixture through meat grinder and cut sausages as desired.

These sausages freeze well.

RAGOÛT DE PATTES ET BOULETTES
Pig's Feet and Meatball Ragout

In old Quebec cookbooks, I noticed that there was a recipe for meat ragout and another for meatballs ragout. Meat ragout was prepared with two or three kinds of meat such as pork, veal and beef while ground pork was the main ingredient in meatballs ragoût. Today, the classic recipe for Quebec "ragoût de pattes" combines meat and meatballs in one dish. Sometimes, leftover chicken is added to the ragout at the end of cooking.

I learned from my grandmother that if you use the pig's back feet, instead of the front feet, you will get more meat. I suggest you proceed with step 1 and 2 one day ahead; it is easier to degrease the broth that way. Ragoût can be placed in refrigerator for 4 days; it also freezes well.

2	pig feet cut in three pieces	2
1	onion	1
1	stalk of celery	1
1 tsp	pickling spices	5 ml
3	cloves	3
2 lb	ground pork or half pork half veal	1 kg
1	egg	1
1/4 tsp	ground nutmeg	1 ml
1/2 tsp	ground cinnamon	2 ml
1/2 tsp	ground cloves	2 ml
1	medium onion, finely chopped	1
	Salt and pepper	
1 cup	all purpose flour	250 ml

1. Put pig feet in a large pot. Cover with cold water, bring to boil and skim. Add onion, celery, pickling spices and simmer for

four hours.

2. Cool to room temperature. Place in refrigerator until fat is set on top of broth. Grill flour in a shallow saucepan at 350°F (175°C); stir flour once in a while until you get a nice amber color, close to peanut butter. Set aside to thicken ragout.

3. Take out casserole from refrigerator. With slotted spoon, remove solid fat on top.

4. Place casserole on medium heat; when liquid is warm, remove pig feet and vegetables from broth and set aside.

5. Mix together, the ground pork, onion, egg, nutmeg, cinnamon, cloves, salt and pepper.

6. Bring broth to a boil, shape ground meat mixture into meat balls and drop them, one by one into the broth. Cover and simmer meatballs for 30 minutes.

7. Remove meatballs from casserole. Bring broth to boil, and whisk in grilled flour, mixed with cold water for pouring consistency. Simmer 30 minutes. Add more grilled flour or a little cornstarch with cold water if the sauce is not thick enough.

8. Remove meat from pig feet and add to the casserole along with meatballs. Simmer 15 minutes to reheat meats.

9. Serve ragoût with boiled potatoes and beets.

> Flour can be grilled on top of the stove. Place flour in a large cast iron skillet and cook on a moderate heat, stirring constantly with a fork until the flour is the colour of peanut butter.

SERVES 8 TO 10

CÔTELETTES DE PORC À L'ÉRABLE
Maple Pork Chops

In Montcalm's diary (an important historic personage), it is mentioned that the French people produced pork of a better quality than did the English. The French used domestic food to feed the pigs while the English just let theirs wander in the woods to find food. In the following recipe, I have suggested a substitute for maple sugar; one should understand that the flavor of the dish won't be the same with brown sugar.

4	pork chops, 3/4 inch thick (2 cm)	4
2 tbsp	butter	30 ml
1/2 tsp	salt	2 ml
1/4 tsp	pepper	1 ml
2 tbsp	all purpose flour	30 ml
1/4 cup	maple sugar or substitute brown sugar	65 ml
2/3 cup	apple juice	175 ml

1. Sauté chops in butter until brown color on both sides.
2. Season with salt and pepper
3. Mix together flour and maple sugar. Sprinkle on chops and add apple juice.
4. Cover and cook for 40 minutes at 350°F (175°C). Toward the end of cooking, remove fat that accumulates in the casserole.

SERVES 4

FRICASSÉE À LA SAUCISSE
Fricassed Sausages

"Fricassée" prepared in Quebec is a much simpler version than its counterpart in Europe. In Quebec, "fricassée" is prepared with cooked meat instead of raw meat as in Europe. Early inhabitants of Quebec must have kept the word "fricassée" since they used a similar method as European cooks to prepare the dish.

If possible, use old potatoes; potatoes will release their starch and thicken the broth into a sauce as it cooks. See index for other "fricassée" recipes prepared with leftover meat.

1 lb	homemade or country sausages	454 g
2 cups	coarsely chopped onions	500 ml
4 cups	diced raw potatoes (½ inch (2cm))	1 litre
1 tsp	dried savory	5 ml
	Salt and pepper to taste	

1. In a large cast iron skillet, cook sausage on medium heat. Set aside cooked sausages.
2. Remove all but 3 tbsp (45 ml) of pan drippings.
3. Sauté onions and diced potatoes in pan drippings until onions are soft and transparent.
4. Cover onions and potatoes with cold water. Cut each sausage into one inch (3 cm) pieces; add to skillet along with seasoning.
5. Bring to boil, cover and simmer for half an hour or until potatoes are cooked.

> Fricassed sausages don't reheat well because of the potatoes.

SERVES 4

TOURTIÈRE DU SAGUENAY
Deep Dish Meat Pie

"Tourtière" is one of my favorite Quebec dishes. It has lots of flavor and reheats well. Although frozen dishes containing potatoes usually lose their flavor, I have found that freezing "Tourtière" doesn't change its flavor. "Tourtière" is an old dish that is very popular in the Saguenay-Lac-St-Jean area. In Quebec, Saguenay-Lac-St-Jean cooks have the reputation for preparing delicious "Tourtières"; every cook has his own way to prepare it. A large "Tourtière" of 25 serving is often cooked for big parties. It's usually prepared with meat and some game but you can prepare a good one without game. Game used can be either wildfowl, venison or hare. A good "Tourtière" should have one part veal, one part pork, and one part game or beef.

I suggest that you serve "Tourtière" after a day of outdoor activities. Prepare meat and onion mixture and cut the potatoes the night before you plan to serve the "tourtière"; the next morning, proceed with the other steps and bake the "Tourtière" all day long.

1 lb	pork shoulder	454 g
1 lb	beef, venison or boned wildfowl meat	454 g
1 lb	veal shoulder	454 g
6	medium onions, chopped	6
4	big potatoes	4
3 tsp	salt	15 ml
1 tsp	pepper	5 ml
3	recipes for pie dough (see index)	
	Eggwash	

1. With hand or electric mincer, mince up meats using perforated cutting disc for coarse mincing. If you don't own a

coarse cutting disc, meat should be cut by hand in $^1/_2$ inch (1 cm) cubes.

2. In a large bowl, combine meats, chopped onions, salt and pepper. Mix well with your hands. Cover with plastic wrap and place in refrigerator overnight.

3. Peel potatoes and cut in $^1/_4$ inch (0,5 cm) cubes. Soak immediately in cold water. Place in refrigerator overnight.

4. The next morning, prepare pie dough. Line one 4 quart casserole or two 2 quart casseroles with pie dough.

5. Remove potatoes from water and keep the water. Combine potato with meat mixture. Fill pastry lined casserole with meat and potatoes. Leave space to seal top crust. Pour potato water into meat mixture; water level should be the same as meat level. If you don't have enough potato water use additional cold tap water.

6. Brush edge of crust with eggwash, cover with topcrust and seal. In center of "tourtière", cut a 2 inches (5 cm) hole. Shape a chimney around your fingers with a narrow piece of foil. Insert chimney in pastry hole and seal chimney with a narrow piece of dough sealed with eggwash.

7. Bake at 350°F (175°C) for one hour and then for 6 hours at 250°F (125°C). By the end of cooking, you should see liquid in the chimney. If there is none, you can add a little hot water into chimney.

> Frozen "tourtière" can be reheated at 250°F (125°C) for about 3 hours if using a 2 quart casserole. A knife inserted into the center of the "tourtière" should feel warm when touching the inside of your forearm.

SERVES 8 TO 10

PATÉ À LA VIANDE
Meatpie

Every family has its own recipe for meatpie. Some like their meatpie prepared only with pork while others use pork and veal. Some like to add spices while others prefer to omit seasoning. Here is my own recipe for meatpie. It's an adaptation from my mother-in-law's recipe.

1 lb	boned pork shoulder	454 g
1	clove of garlic, finely chopped	1
1	medium potato, peeled	1
1	small onion, chopped	1
1 cup	boiling water	250 ml
$^1/_4$ tsp	dry mustard	1 ml
$^1/_4$ tsp	pepper	1 ml
$^1/_4$ tsp	ground clove	1 ml
$^1/_4$ tsp	ground cinnanon	1 ml
	Pie dough for two crusts (see index)	
	Salt	
	Dry bread crumbs as needed	
	Eggwash	

1. Grind meat in meat grinder.
2. Place ground meat into a medium casserole, insert peeled potato into meat, add boiling water, onion, mustard, pepper, cloves, and cinnamon. Bring to boil and simmer until potato is cooked. This will take about $1^1/_2$ hour.
3. Remove potato from casserole, mash and return it to the casserole. Mix meat and potato well.
4. Season with salt. If mixture seem too liquid, add bread crumbs; it should have a consistency of thick meat spaghetti sauce.

5. Cool completely. Meat mixture can be prepared one or two days ahead; place mixture in refrigerator until ready to use.
6. Prepare pie dough.
7. Line a 9 inch (23 cm) pie plate with pie dough; fill with meat mixture and cover with top crust sealing both crusts with eggwash.
8. Slit and brush top crust with eggwash.
9. Cook at 400°F (220°C) for 15 minutes and then for 20 minutes at 350°F (175°C).

> Meatpie freezes well. To defrost, place in a 350°F (175°C) oven for about one hour.

SERVES 4

CROQUETTES DE JAMBON
Ham Croquettes

2 cups	leftover cooked ham, finely chopped	500 ml
2	eggs	2
2 cups	mashed potatoes	500 ml
1/2 tsp	powdered beef base	3 ml
1 tbsp	chopped onion	15 ml
1 tsp	parsley either dried or fresh	5 ml
	Salt and pepper	
	Bacon fat for cooking	

1. In a large bowl, mix all ingredients except bacon fat.
2. Shape croquettes the size of a hamburger.
3. Melt bacon fat in a cast iron skillet. Cook croquettes on medium heat until brown on both sides.

SERVES 4

BOUDIN EN SAUCE BLANCHE
Blood Pudding in White Sauce

4 tbsp	butter	60 ml
4 tbsp	all purpose flour	60 ml
2 cups	milk	500 ml
	Salt and pepper	
2	medium onions, sliced	2
1/4 tsp	ground cloves	1 ml
4	blood pudding pieces	4
	Butter to cook blood pudding	

1. In a medium skillet, cook blood pudding in butter on low heat; cover skillet to prevent blood pudding from becoming dry.
2. In a medium casserole, melt butter and cook onions until transparent but not brown. Add flour and mix well; simmer one minute.
3. With whisk, incorporate milk. Bring to boil and simmer until thickened.
4. Season with salt, pepper and cloves.
5. Remove skin from blood pudding.
6. To serve, pour sauce on top of blood pudding.
7. Serve with boiled potatoes.

SERVES 4

LARD SALÉ
Salted Pork

Here, I explain how salted pork is prepared for those who wouldn't be able to buy it in their area. Thanks to my butcher Mr. Jacques Pothier for sharing his recipe. Salted pork will keep for one year.

Coarse salt
Cold water
Pork back fat with or without meat
One large wooden or plastic container

1. For brine, mix together 1 part salt to 3 parts water and stir for 10 minutes. If the mixture contains enough salt, a raw egg (in its shell) will float when dropped into the mixture.
2. Cut pork fat into 4 inch (10 cm) squares. Dip each piece of pork in salt so that all sides are covered with salt.
3. Place a layer of pork into the container and sprinkle with more salt.
4. Repeat step 3 until you have no more pieces of pork.
5. Pour brine on top of pork; it should completely cover pork. If using steaked pork fat, pour off brine after 3 weeks and add new brine to the pork.

Pig's Feet and Meatball Ragout

Picturesque Charlevoix scenery

Charlevoix outdoor bread oven

BEEF AND VEAL

Except for the past decade, beef was served well done most of the time. Tender cuts of beef were used for steaks, cooked in butter in a cast iron skillet. Less tender cuts were used for stews or dishes prepared with ground beef.

Veal wasn't a very popular meat; it was often overcooked and hard to chew. The only tasty veal I happened to have liked in my childhood was veal roast braised with pork roast which my grandmother cooked together in the same casserole. That way, the fat melting from the pork probably tenderized the veal.

RÔTI DE BOEUF ET PATATES BRUNES
Braised Beef with Browned Potatoes

If you prefer, you can cook this dish in the oven. Cook for 4 hours at 300°F (165°C); add potatoes one hour before the end of cooking. If beef is ready before potatoes, remove from casserole and wrap in foil to keep warm. Raise oven temperature to cook potatoes. This dish will have a better flavor if cooked in a cast iron casserole.

4 lb	*beef shoulder*	2 kg
2	*large onions, coarsely chopped*	2
4	*slices salted pork*	4
	Salt and pepper	
10	*small peeled potatoes*	10

1. Melt salted pork in a large heavy casserole. Remove pork slices.
2. Brown beef on all sides in melted fat.
3. Add onions and sauté until golden.
4. Season with salt and pepper. Add salted pork slices and one cup (250 ml) boiling water to the kettle. Cover and cook on low heat for two hours. Add water if necessary; there should be at least one cup of liquid in the casserole.
5. Add potatoes one hour before the end of cooking. When potatoes are half done, turn them over.
6. To check if beef is done, insert a long-tined fork into the meat: roast should fall back in casserole when lifted.

SERVES 8 TO 10

GIBELOTTE AU BOEUF
Meatballs and Vegetable Stew

This dish is delicious and easy to prepare; it also reheats well. I am indebted to my friend Mireille Dauth who shared her mother's recipe; it's a favorite in her family.

2 lb	ground beef	1 kg
1	large onion, sliced	1
4	potatoes, sliced	4
4	carrots, sliced	4
1	10 oz (300 ml) tomato soup can	1
1	19 oz (600 ml) tomato juice can	1
	Salt and Pepper	
	A pinch of sugar	
1/2 cup	water	125 ml

1. Shape ground beef into 2 inch (5 cm) meatballs.
2. Place meatballs in a large oven casserole, cover first with sliced onions, next sliced carrots and finish with sliced potatoes.
3. Pour tomato soup, tomato juice and water on top of meat and vegetables.
4. Season with salt, pepper and a pinch of sugar.
5. Cover and cook at 350°F (175°C) for 2 hours or until vegetables are done.

SERVES 4 TO 6

BOUILLI DE BOEUF ET LÉGUMES
Boiled Beef and Vegetables

In summer, people wait for fresh vegetables to prepare the "Bouilli de boeuf et légumes". Except for the potatoes, the flavor of "Bouilli" improves when reheated. Some cooks boil the cabbage in a different casserole and add it to the "bouilli" just before serving; I personally prefer to have the cabbage cooked in the "bouilli". For a faster service, you can tie beans into bundles before adding to the casserole.

4 lb	beef shoulder, chuck or blade	2 kg
4	whole peppercorns	4
8 cups	cold water	2 litres
1	unpeeled carrot	1
1	large onion	1
1/4 tsp	dried thyme	1 ml
1	bay leaf	1
2 tsp	salt	10 ml
1	slice of salt pork (optional)	1
8	peeled carrots	8
1 lb	green or wax beans	454 g
8	potatoes	8
1	small turnip, sliced 1 inch (2 cm) thick	1
1	green cabbage, quartered	1

1. In a large kettle, bring water to boil. Add peppercorn, unpeeled carrot, onion, thyme, bay leaf and salt. Boil for 5 minutes.
2. Add beef and salt pork to the broth; cover and simmer 4 hours or until meat is tender.
3. One hour before the end of cooking, add carrots, beans, potatoes and turnip to the kettle.

4. Half an hour before the end of cooking, add cabbage to the "bouilli".

> "Bouilli" will keep well for 5 days in the refrigerator.

SERVES 8

FRICASSÉE DE BOEUF
Beef Fricassee

Although cooked potatoes can be used to prepare this dish, "Fricassée" has a better flavor if made with raw potatoes.

$1/3$ cup	cooking fat from beef or shortening	125 ml
2 cups	leftover beef, cut in small cubes	500 ml
2 cups	chopped onions	500 ml
4 cups	peeled potatoes, diced	1 litre
1 tsp	dry savory	5 ml
	Beef broth from cooking and water as needed	
	Salt and pepper	

1. Melt fat, preferably in a cast iron skillet.
2. Sauté onions and potatoes until golden brown.
3. Add beef and seasoning, cover with beef broth and water.
4. Simmer covered, for 30 minutes or until potatoes are cooked.

SERVES 4

PAIN DE VIANDE AUX TOMATES DE MAMAN

Mummy's Tomato Meatloaf

You'll get a meatloaf with a sauce in one dish. It's also very good if baked in the microwave.

1 lb	ground beef	454 g
1	small onion, chopped	1
1	10 oz (300 ml) tomato soup can	1
1/2 cup	milk	125 ml
1/2 cup	dry breadcrumbs or quick cooking oatmeal	125 ml
1	egg	1
	Salt and pepper	

1. Mix all ingredients except tomato soup.
2. Pour mixture into a bread pan or into a glassware casserole if cooked in the microwave.
3. Mix tomato soup with 1/2 cup (125 ml) cold water. Pour on top of meatloaf.
4. Cook for one hour at 350°F (175°C).
5. If using a microwave, reduce water to 1/3 cup (90 ml), cover and microwave at 80% for 10 minutes, turn dish and microwave for another 10 minutes at 80%; let stand for 5 minutes before serving.

SERVES 4

PÂTÉ CHINOIS
Quebec Sheperd's Pie

This is the French Canadian version of Sheperd's pie. Québécois opinions vary on the way their Sheperd's pie should be prepared; some prefer it prepared with "old" while others prefer it with "new". "Old" means it's prepared with leftover cooked beef, and "new" means it's prepared with fresh ground beef. My children prefer Sheperd's pie prepared with "new" but I prefer mine with "old"; I think it has more flavor.

2 cups	leftover cooked beef with cooking juice OR 1 lb (454 g) ground beef	500 ml
1	14 oz (412 ml) creamed corn can	1
3 cups	mashed potatoes	750 ml
	Paprika	

1. If using leftover beef, grind and mix with cooking juice. If using ground beef, sauté in vegetable oil or butter.
2. Place meat in an oven casserole, cover with creamed corn and finish with mashed potatoes.
3. Sprinkle with paprika.
4. Bake for about 45 minutes at 350°F (175°C).
5. Serve with homemade ketchup and pickles.

SERVES 4

Beef Roll

Meat mixture

1¹/₂ lb	ground beef	675 g
1	medium onion, chopped	1
1 tbsp	butter	15 ml
2 tbsp	chopped green pepper	30 ml
1 tsp	brown basting sauce	5 ml

Dough

2 cups	flour	500 ml
4 tsp	baking powder	20 ml
¹/₂ tsp	salt	3 ml
¹/₄ cup	shortening	60 ml
³/₄ to 1 cup	milk	175 to 250 ml

Sauce

2 tbsp	butter	30 ml
2 tbsp	flour	30 ml
1	19 oz (600ml) seasoned tomatoes can	1
1 cup	tomato juice	250 ml
1 tsp	sugar	5 ml
	Salt and pepper	

1. Sauté onion in melted butter in a large skillet. Add meat and green pepper and cook completely. Drain excess liquid.
2. Add brown basting sauce to meat mixture and set aside to cool
3. In a medium bowl, mix flour, baking powder and salt. Blend shortening, with your fingertips or pastry blender, into flour mixture. Add milk and gather into a ball. This operation can be done in a food processor; don't overmix or it will toughen the dough.
4. Roll dough into a rectangular shape, ¹/₄ inch (1 cm) thick.
5. Spread cooled meat mixture onto the dough. Brush edges of

dough with eggwash.

6. Roll, starting with the long sides; seal ends and place roll on a cookie sheet sealed side down.

7. Bake for 20 minutes at 400°F (220°C) or until golden brown.

8. Prepare sauce while roll is baking. Melt butter in a medium casserole, add flour and cook on very low heat for 1 minute. Add crushed tomatoes, tomato juice, sugar, salt and pepper. Bring to boil and simmer until sauce thickens. Stir sauce a few times while simmering.

9. To serve, cut roll in 1 inch (2 cm) slices and pour sauce on top.

SERVES 4 TO 6

Meatballs in Chicken Broth

1 lb	lean ground beef	454 g
1	egg, beaten	1
1	small onion, finely chopped	1
3/4 cup	dry bread crumbs	175 ml
1/4 cup	milk	45 ml
1/4 cup	heavy cream	45 ml
	Salt and pepper	
	A pinch of nutmeg	
	Homemade chicken broth	

1. Blend together, beef, egg, onion, breadcrumbs, milk, heavy cream, salt, pepper and nutmeg.
2. Shape into meatballs.
3. Bring chicken broth to boil and drop meatballs in broth one by one. Lower heat and simmer for 30 minutes. If desired, sprinkle with fresh chopped parsley.
4. Serve in soup bowls. Salad and fresh bread are good complements for a light lunch.

SERVES 4

FRICADELLES DE VEAU ET DE PORC
Veal and Pork Patties

³/₄ lb	ground veal	375 g
¹/₄ lb	ground pork	125 g
³/₄ cup	fresh bread crumbs	175 ml
¹/₄ cup	milk	60 ml
1	small clove of garlic, crushed finely	1
1	egg	1
	Salt and pepper	
	All purpose flour	
2 tbsp	butter	30 ml
2 tbsp	shortening	30 ml

1. Soak breadcrumbs in milk.
2. Mix together, ground meats, garlic, egg, soaked bread, salt and pepper.
3. Shape meat mixture into patties; coat patties with flour, shaking off excess flour.
4. Melt shortening and butter in skillet. Cook patties on each sides until well done.
5. Remove patties from skillet and keep warm. Pour off excess fat, add ¹/₂ cup (125 ml) water to skillet, scrape skillet and reduce cooking juice by half. Pour juice on patties.
6. Serve with mashed potatoes and vegetable of your choice.

SERVES 4

POULTRY

BOUILLI DE POULET
Boiled Chicken and Vegetables

Previously, hens were used to prepare this dish. Since hens are more difficult to find at the supermarket, I buy a large utility grade chicken which is less expensive than a first grade chicken.

1	6 lb (3 kg) utility chicken	1
	Salt and pepper	
1/4 tsp	thyme	1 ml
1	clove of garlic, crushed	1
1/4 tsp	nutmeg	1 ml
1/2	lemon	1/2
2	chopped onions	2
3	slices streaky salt pork	3
1/2 tsp	dry savory	2 ml
	A pinch ground cloves	
15	whole carrots	15
6	peeled potatoes	6
1 lb	wax beans	454 g
1	green cabbage, cut in wedges	1

1. Remove all visible fat from chicken. Season with salt and pepper and put thyme and garlic in chicken cavity.
2. Rub chicken with lemon and nutmeg.
3. In a large casserole, melt enough chicken fat to sauté chicken on all sides. Set chicken aside and sauté onion until transparent.
4. Put chicken back in casserole along with salt pork, savory and cloves. Add water just covering the chicken, cover and simmer for 2 hours.
5. Add vegetables and cook for one hour or until vegetables are tender.

SERVES 6

Roast Chicken and Meatballs

In my childhood, this was a family favorite usually served on Sundays. My mother, to our request, served it with boiled white rice soaked with plenty of cooking juices. The meatballs cooked around the chicken absorb extra flavor from the chicken cooking juices. If you have unexpected guests, this dish comes in handy to extend the number of servings for your meal.

1	3 to 4 lb (1.5 to 2 kg) roasting chicken	1
	Salt and pepper	
1	medium onion, sliced	1
2 tbsp	butter	30 ml
1 tbsp	dry mustard	15 ml
1 lb	ground beef	454 g
1	egg	1
1/2 cup	dry breadcrumbs	125 ml

1. Heat oven to 350°F (175°C).
2. Lay onion slices on the bottom of a shallow roasting pan large enough to contain chicken with meatballs placed around chicken.
3. Season chicken with salt and pepper. Mix butter with dry mustard well. Cover chicken with mustard butter and place chicken on top of onions.
4. Roast uncovered, for 2 hours, baste every 15 minutes if possible.

5. While chicken is roasting, prepare meatballs. Mix together ground beef, egg, dry breadcrumbs, salt and pepper. Shape mixture into meatballs.
6. Forty five minutes before end of cooking, arrange meatballs around chicken, turning once when half-cooked. If there is not enough liquid in the pan, you can add a little water; there should be about $^3/_4$ inch (2 cm) of cooking juice.
7. Serve with rice and green vegetables.

SERVES 6

POULET GRATINÉ
Chicken au Gratin

6	chicken breasts	6
2	eggs	2
³/₄ cup	all purpose flour	190 ml
	Salt and pepper	
2 tbsp	butter	30 ml
2 tbsp	vegetable oil	30 ml
1¹/₂ cups	chicken broth	375 ml
1	green pepper diced	1
1³/₄ cups	peeled, seeded and sliced tomatoes	400 ml
³/₄ cup	heavy cream	190 ml
2 tbsp	all purpose flour	30 ml
2 tbsp	cold water	30 ml
2 cups	grated gruyère cheese	500 ml

1. Dip chicken in beaten eggs and coat with flour shaking off excess.
2. Sauté in melted butter and oil until golden brown.
3. Lay sauté chicken breasts in an oven casserole. Add chicken broth and pepper; cover and bake for 30 minutes at 350°F (175°C).
4. Remove chicken breast from casserole and boil cooking juice for 5minutes. Add tomatoes and cook for another 3 minutes.
5. Remove vegetables from cooking juice. Add cream and mix well.
6. Mix the 2 tbsp of flour with cold water and pour in cooking juice to thicken. Simmer sauce for 15 minutes.
7. Pour sauce on top of chicken breasts and vegetables, cover with cheese and broil until brown.

SERVES 6

GAME

Hunting is a very popular sport in Quebec. In colonial times, farmers hunted for survival. They learned from the Natives which game were good to eat and how to prepare it. As the years passed, even though they didn't need to rely on game anymore, Québécois are still fond of game dishes.

Today, if one does not hunt, then they must be invited to a hunter's table in order to savor a wild game meal. The most popular types of wild game in Quebec are wild duck, hare, partridge, moose and deer.

RÔTI D'ORIGNAL
Moose Roast

The flavor of moose is especially good if it comes from a young animal.

3 lb	moose roast (tender cut)	1,5 kg
4 tbsp	butter	60 ml
1 tbsp	dry mustard	15 ml
	Salt and pepper	
	Parsley	
	A pinch of thyme	
1	medium sliced onion	1
4 oz	dry red wine	125 ml

1. Heat oven to 400°F (220°C).
2. Sprinkle roast with salt and pepper.
3. Mix butter and mustard together. Spread this mixture onto the lean parts of the roast.
4. Place onion slices in the bottom of a shallow roasting pan. Lay roast on onion slices and sprinkle with parsley and thyme.
5. Cook roast for 10 minutes, lower heat to 350°F (175°C), and cook for :
   - 18 min./ lb (0,5 kg) for rare
   - 20 min./ lb (0,5 kg) for medium
   - 22 min./ lb (0,5 kg) for well done
6. Do not cover roast while roasting; baste every 15 minutes.
7. Fifteen minutes before end of cooking, add wine.
8. To serve, pour cooking juices on slices of roast.

SERVES 6

PERDRIX À LA CRÈME
Creamed Partridge

This old recipe is absolutely delicious and yet, so easy to prepare. I usually serve this dish with a casserole of white and wild rice and a green vegetable such as broccoli.

2	*partridges*	2
2 tbsp	*butter*	30 ml
2 cups	*heavy cream*	500 ml
	Salt and pepper	

1. Season partridges with salt and pepper.
2. Melt butter in a medium casserole and brown partridges on each side on medium heat.
3. Pour a small amount of cream on top of partridges.
4. Cook partridges uncovered for 2 hours at 350°F (175°C). Baste partridges every 15 minutes adding more of the cream. Keep a third of the cream to finish sauce at the end of cooking.
5. Remove partridges from casserole and let sit for 5 minutes before slicing.
6. Pour leftover cream into casserole, scrape casserole with spatula, bring to boil and cook until sauce is slightly thick. Season sauce and add sliced partridge to the sauce.

> Cooked partridge carcasses can be used later to prepare "Cream of partridge".

SERVES 3

PERDRIX AU COGNAC FLAMBÉ
Cognac Flambé Partridge

This dish is also delicious when prepared with chicken breasts.

2	partridges, breasts deboned	2
3 tbsp	butter	45 ml
2 tbsp	cognac	30 ml
2	chopped shallots	2
¹/₂ lb	sliced mushrooms	225 g
1 tbsp	flour	15 ml
¹/₂ cup	dry white wine	125 ml
1 cup	heavy cream	250 ml
	Salt and pepper	

1. In a skillet, sauté breasts of partridge in butter, 5 minutes on each side.
2. Remove fat from skillet and save for later.
3. Add cognac and ignite to flambé partridges. Remove partridges from skillet.
4. Put saved cooking fat back into skillet and sauté shallots and mushrooms.
5. Add flour and mix well with vegetables. Add wine and boil to reduce volume by half.
6. Add cream and simmer for a few minutes.
7. Add breasts of partridge to skillet, cover and cook on low heat for 10 minutes. Season the sauce and check for consistency. If too watery you can add a small amount of cornstarch mixed with a little bit of cold water. Let simmer for 2 minutes.

SERVES *4*

FÈVES AU LARD À LA PERDRIX
Beans and Partridges

Some people use hare instead of partridge to prepare this dish; the choice is yours, depending which of these two you prefer. The game meat is buried in the pork and beans. The beans get extra flavor from game and the latter, which is fairly lean, absorbs some of the pork fat which results in a tender and juicy meat.

2 cups	dry pinto beans	500 ml
$^1/_2$ lb	salted pork	225 g
$1^1/_2$ tsp	dry mustard	7 ml
1	medium onion	1
	A pinch of thyme	
$^1/_2$ cup	brown sugar	125 ml
$^1/_4$ cup	molasses	60 ml
	Salt and pepper	
	Breasts of two partridges	

1. Wash and soak beans for 6 to 8 hours.
2. Bring beans to boil, cook rapidly for 10 minutes. Drain and rinse under cold water.
3. Place beans in a thick oven casserole, add salted pork cut in big pieces, thyme, brown sugar and molasses. Season with salt and pepper and cover with water.
4. Bury breasts of partridge, meaty side in center of beans.
5. Cover and cook at 250°F (120°C) for 7 to 8 hours.

SERVES 6 TO 8

PERDRIX AU CHOU
Partridge with Cabbage

2	partridges, breasts only	2
	All purpose flour	
1/4 lb	salted pork	125 g
1	small green cabbage, coarsely chopped	1
2	onions, sliced	2
1 tsp	salt	5 ml
1/4 tsp	pepper	1 ml
1/4 tsp	thyme	1 ml
1 cup	dry white wine	250 ml

1. Cut salted pork into small cubes, place in a small saucepan and cover with cold water. Bring to a boil, drain and rinse in cold water.
2. Melt salted pork in a large oven casserole. Cut each partridge in two pieces, coat with flour shaking off excess flour and sauté in melted fat until brown.
3. Remove partridges from casserole and set aside. Add cabbage and onions to casserole, mix well with pork fat, cover and cook on medium heat for 15 minutes, stirring often.
4. Place pieces of partridge on top of cabbage and add salt, pepper, thyme and wine, cover and cook for 2 hours at 350°F (175°C).

SERVES 4

FAISAN EN CASSEROLE
Braised Pheasant

I am grateful to Mrs Georgette Descôteaux for sharing this old family recipe. This is certainly the most delicious pheasant dish I ever tasted. It is also very easy to prepare.

1/2	bottle dry red wine	1/2
2 tsp	savory	10 ml
2 tsp	parsley	10 ml
1	medium carrot shredded	1
1/2 lb	salted pork	225 g
2	pheasants	2

1. In a large bowl, mix together, wine, savory, parsley and carrots. Add pheasants and marinate for 5 to 8 hours in refrigerator.
2. Slice salted pork and melt in a heavy casserole.
3. Remove pheasants from marinade, pat dry with paper towels and sauté in melted fat until pale brown.
4. Pour some of the marinade on pheasants, cover and cook for 3 hours at 350°F (175°C). Baste meat frequently with more marinade.

SERVES 4 TO 6

TOURTIÈRE DU SAGUENAY
Saguenay Meat and Game Pie

See Pork chapter

EGGS

OMELETTE AUX OREILLES DE CRISSE
Salted Pork Omelette

8	eggs	8
8	slices salted pork streaked with meat	8
¹/₃ cup	milk	75 ml
	Pepper to taste	

1. Remove rind from salted pork.
2. Place salted pork in a small casserole, cover with cold water, bring to boil, drain and rinse pork under cold water.
3. Place slices of salted pork in a medium skillet, and cook uncovered on medium heat until brown and crisp. Turn slices over a few times while cooking.
4. Mix eggs, milk and pepper well.
5. Remove fat from skillet except 2 tbsp (30 ml).
6. Pour egg mixture on top of cooked salted pork and cook on medium heat until there is no trace of liquid.
7. Serve immediately

SERVES **4**

OEUFS DURS EN SAUCE AUX OIGNONS
Eggs in a White Onion Sauce

6	hard boiled eggs	6
4	medium onions	4
2 tbsp	butter	30 ml
	A pinch of thyme	
1/2 tsp	salt	2 ml
	A pinch of nutmeg	
	A pinch of pepper	
1 tbsp	parsley	15 ml
3 tbsp	flour	45 ml
1 cup	milk	250 ml
1 cup	cream	250 ml
3	bread slices, toasted and cut in triangles	3

1. Preheat oven to 450°F (230°C). Cut onions in thin slices.
2. Melt butter in a medium saucepan and cook onions, thyme, nutmeg, salt and pepper until transparent.
3. Add flour, mix well and cook on low heat for 2 minutes. Add parsley.
4. Add milk and cream, mix well, bring to boil and simmer for about 5 minutes until thickened.
5. Quarter eggs, place in an oven casserole, pour sauce on top of eggs and place in oven for about 5 minutes or until sauce bubbles. Serve with toast triangles.

SERVES 6

OEUFS DANS LE VINAIGRE
Pickled Eggs

This is the way Québécois like their pickled eggs; no spices to flavor the eggs, only plain white vinegar and water.

> Hard boiled eggs
> Cold water
> White vinegar

1. Marinate the eggs at least 6 hours in a solution of half vinegar, half water or 1/3 vinegar, 2/3 water depending on your taste. Serve with crackers.

VEGETABLES

Before the refrigerator was invented, there were not many kinds of vegetables on the Québécois menu. Due to the short summer season, mainly cool weather vegetables (carrots, potatoes, cabbage, etc...) were cultivated. Fresh vegetables such as lettuce, cucumber, beans and corn were eaten during the summer and early autumn. In winter and spring, they had to rely on pickles and root vegetables such as potatoes, carrots, turnips and beets which were kept in an outdoor root cellar. Today, Québécois eat all kinds of vegetables offered on the market.

POMMES DE TERRE ET CAROTTES EN PURÉE
Mashed Potatoes and Carrots

This potato dish was a favorite in my family. When I was young, my mother shaped these colorful potatoes into small square cakes. As I grew older, I didn't bother shaping them and found that they are just as tasty and colorful as I remember them.

3	medium potatoes	3
4	medium carrots	4
	Milk	
1 tbsp	butter	15 ml
	Salt and pepper to taste	

1. Peel potatoes and carrots and cook in salted water until tender. Drain water.
2. Mash carrots and potatoes together, add butter. Add milk until you get a nice purée. Quantity of milk used depend on kind of potatoes used.
3. Season with salt and pepper.

SERVES 3 TO 4

PATATES RÔTIES
Roast Potatoes

My children love these crusty potatoes. They are prepared with leftover boiled potatoes sliced 1/4 inch (1 cm) thick and fried on both sides in melted shortening in a black iron skillet. They are ready when golden brown in color on both sides. Drain on paper towels.

CHOU ET OIGNONS SAUTÉS
Sauteed Cabbage and Onions

2 tbsp	*butter*	*30 ml*
1	*small green cabbage sliced*	*1*
1	*small onion chopped*	*1*
	Salt and pepper	

1. Melt butter in a large skillet.
2. Add sliced cabbage and onion and sauté until golden.
3. Season with salt and pepper, cover and simmer until tender. Stir a few times during cooking.

SERVES *4*

DESSERTS

Desserts have always played an important role in Quebecers' menus. Quebecers are very fond of desserts and like them sweet and preferably warm. Except for the famous Bûche de Noël, desserts are very simple to prepare.

The most popular types of desserts are pies, galettes, puddings and cakes which are often accompanied by a sauce.

GÂTEAU AU BEURRE

Butter Cake

I always loved to watch my grandmother prepare this cake. She didn't bother measuring ingredients and her cake was always delicious with the same texture. It took me years to understand that she had learned to judge a batter by the texture. I usually freeze half, without frosting, for future use.

3 cups	cake and pastry flour	725 ml
3 tsp	baking powder	15 ml
1/2 tsp	salt	2 ml
1 cup	soft butter	250 ml
2 cups	white sugar	500 ml
1 tsp	vanilla	5 ml
4	large eggs	4
1 cup	milk	250 ml

1. Grease three round cake molds or 2 round cake tins and 6 cupcakes. Cover bottom of molds with wax paper.
2. Sieve flour before measuring.
3. Sieve measured flour with baking powder and salt. Set aside.
4. Cream butter, sugar and vanilla for 10 minutes.
5. Add eggs one at a time, beat well after each addition.
6. Add flour mixture alternating with milk, beginning and ending with flour.
7. Pour batter into molds and cook in the middle of the oven for about 30 to 35 minutes or until a toothpick inserted into cake comes out clean.
8. Cool 5 minutes and unmold. Let cool on wire racks.

Pork Roast and Yellow Potatoes (p.51)

Sainte-Anne-de-la-Pérade tommy cod fishing cabins
in the Mauricie region

Bags of frozen tommy cods for sale

GÂTEAU AU BEURRE AU SUCRE À LA CRÈME
Buttercake with Penuche Sauce

This dessert is very popular in the Mauricie area. It is my husband's favorite dessert.

	One layer buttercake above	
Penuche sauce		
1 cup	brown sugar	250 ml
1 cup	white sugar	250 ml
1 cup	heavy cream	250 ml
1 tsp	vanilla	5 ml

1. Mix brown and white sugar in a medium saucepan.
2. Add cream and mix well.
3. Bring to boil and simmer for 5 minutes stirring once in a while. Add vanilla.
4. For each portion, place a piece of cake in a deep bowl and pour warm sauce on top of cake.

> Sauce can be reheated on low heat.

SERVES 6 TO 8

GÂTEAU AU CARAMEL

Caramel Cake

This is one of the most delicious cakes I have ever tasted. Special thanks to Mrs. Gilberte Morin Martinson for sharing one of her best family recipes. The recipe for this cake has been handed down from mother to daughter for many generations.

Caramel

1 cup	white sugar	250 ml
1/4 cup	cold water	60 ml
1/2 cup	hot water	125 ml

Cake

2 cups	white sugar	500 ml
3	eggs	3
1/2 cup	butter	125 ml
1 tsp	vanilla	5 ml
1/2	cup milk	125 ml
3 cups	flour	625 ml
3 tsp	baking powder	15 ml
1/2 tsp	salt	2 ml

1. For the caramel, place the cup of sugar and cold water in a saucepan on low heat. Cook until caramel becomes a nice amber color. Remove from heat, add hot water stirring with a long handed wooden spoon to stay away from steam and mix well. Set aside to cool.
2. Beat eggs with sugar until the mixture is a lemony color. Add melted butter, vanilla and caramel. Mix well.
3. Blend flour, baking powder and salt and add to the batter alternating with milk.
4. Pour cake batter into a greased 9 x 13 inch (20 x 30 cm) rectangular pan and bake at 350°F (175°C) for 1 to 30 to 40

minutes or until a toothpick inserted in cake comes out clean.

Icing

1 cup	light brown sugar	250 ml
4$^1/_2$ tbsp	butter	67 ml
3 tbsp	milk	45 ml
$^1/_2$ cup	sifted icing sugar	125 ml

1. Place brown sugar, butter and milk into a saucepan. Bring to a boil and cook for 2 minutes on low heat.
2. Remove from heat and blend in sifted icing sugar.
3. Spread cake with icing while still warm.

GÂTEAU AU BEURRE ET SAUCE AU CITRON
Buttercake with Lemon Sauce

One layer of buttercake

Lemon sauce

3 tbsp	lemon juice	45 ml
1¹/₂ tsp	lemon zest	7 ml
¹/₂ cup	sugar	125 ml
2 tbsp	cornstach	30 ml
¹/₄ tsp	salt	1 ml
1 cup	cold water	250 ml
1¹/₂ tbsp	butter	22 ml

1. Mix sugar, cornstarch and salt in a saucepan.
2. Add water, bring to boil and simmer until thickened.
3. Add lemon juice, zest and butter.
4. Place a piece of cake in a deep bowl and cover with warm sauce.

SERVES *4* TO *6*

GÂTEAU À LA MÉLASSE
Molasses Cake

3 cups	sifted flour	675 ml
1 tsp	baking soda	5 ml
3/4 tsp	salt	3 ml
1 tbsp	cinnamon	15 ml
1 1/2 tsp	nutmeg	7 ml
1 cup	soft butter	250 ml
1 cup	sugar	250 ml
3	eggs	3
3/4 cup	molasses	175 ml
1/3 cup	"All Bran" cereal	75 ml
3/4 cup	buttermilk or sour milk	175 ml

1. Sift together flour, baking soda, salt and spices.
2. Cream butter and sugar until light and fluffy.
3. Add eggs.
4. Add dry ingredients alternating with milk.
5. Add cereal and molasses.
6. Pour batter into a greased rectangular pan and cook for 1 to 1 1/2 hour or until a toothpick inserted in cake comes out clean.
7. Serve warm spread with butter.

BÛCHE DE NOËL
Yule Log

The Yule Log is the traditional dessert served at Christmas dinner. It's a tradition that early settlers kept from their homeland France.

4	eggs	4
1 cup	sugar	250 ml
3 tbsp	cold water	45 ml
1 cup	cake flour	250 ml
1¹/₂ tbsp	cornstach	23 ml
1¹/₂ tsp	baking powder	7 ml
¹/₄ tsp	salt	1 ml
¹/₂ tsp	almond extract	2 ml
¹/₂ tsp	vanilla	2 ml
	Chocolate icing of your choice	

1. Grease and cover bottom of a 10 x 15 inch (23 x 38 cm) jelly roll pan with wax paper. Beat eggs until frothy and pale lemon in color.
2. Add sugar and water and beat until batter becomes white.
3. Sift dry ingredients and gently add them to the batter with a spatula.
4. Add vanilla and almond extract and pour batter into pan.
5. Bake in the middle of oven at 400°F (220°C) for 15 minutes.
6. Remove cake from mold while it is still warm, and place on a piece of wax paper sprinkled with white or icing sugar. Roll the cake and let cool on a wire rack.
7. Unroll and fill with jam or buttercream. Roll the cake again and cut a 2 inch slice from one end. Diagonally cut this slice in two and attach these two parts, with a dab of icing, to the side of the jelly roll. By doing so, the jelly roll should have the shape of a log with two knots on the top of it.

8. Cream both ends and top of knots with white icing. Cream the rest of the log with chocolate icing. Run a fork lengthwise through the icing. This will give the log the appearance of true wood. For the knots, and the ends of the log, use the fork again, but this time in a circular motion.

9. If desired, decorate the Yule Log with green leaves made of almond paste and red cherry or small red cinnamon candies.

Small Chocolate Cream Filled Cakes

These small popular commercial cakes called "Jos Louis" originate from Beauce région. The founder of a bakery, Arcade Vachon, named them after both his eldest sons, Joseph and Louis. The Vachon company sells these cakes as far away as New England and Ontario. The following recipe is a homemade version of these cakes. If you wish, you can ice them with a thin chocolate icing.

$^1/_2$ cup	shortening	125 ml
1 cup	sugar	250 ml
2	eggs	2
1 cup	milk	250 ml
1 tsp	vanilla	5 ml
$1^3/_4$ cups	flour	425 ml
2 tsp	baking powder	10 ml
1 tsp	baking soda	5 ml
1 tsp	salt	5 ml
$^1/_4$ cup	cocoa powder	45 ml

1. Cream shortening, beat in sugar. Add eggs and mix well.
2. Add vanilla. Mix flour, baking powder, baking soda, salt and cocoa powder. Alternately add milk to batter.
3. Drop heaping tablespoonful of cake batter on a greased cookie sheet leaving space for cakes to expand while cooking.
4. Bake for 8 to 10 minutes at 350°F (175°C). Cool on wire rack.

Filling

1¹/₃ cups	shortening or half butter half shortening	325 ml
5 tbsp	boiling water	75 ml
5 cups	icing sugar	1,25 litres
1 tsp	vanilla	5 ml

1. Cream shortening and mix in boiling water.
2. Add icing sugar one cup at a time while beating constantly. Add vanilla. Filling should be like mashed potatoes. Spread one cake with filling and top with another.

POUDING DU CHÔMEUR
Poor Man's Pudding

Quebecers are very fond of puddings. This is another example of English influence on Quebec Cuisine. Most of the time, Quebec puddings are prepared with a batter similar to cake batter and baked in the oven. This is what makes them different from English puddings, which are steamed instead of baked in the oven.

Batter		
2 tsp	shortening	10 ml
3/4 cup	sugar	175 ml
1 1/2 tsp	baking powder	7 ml
1/3 cup	milk	75 ml
1	egg	1
1 cup	all purpose flour	250 ml
1/2 tsp	salt	2 ml
1 tsp	vanilla	5 ml
Sauce		
2 cups	brown sugar	500 ml
1/2 cup	chopped nuts (optional)	125 ml
1 cup	water	250 ml
2 tsp	butter	10 ml

1. In a medium bowl, cream shortening, gradually add sugar.
2. Add egg and beat well.
3. Mix flour with salt and baking powder. Add to the batter alternately with milk. Add vanilla.
4. For the sauce, boil brown sugar, water, nuts if used and butter in a casserole for 8 minutes.
5. Pour batter into a pan the size and shape of a bread tin or similar size tin and pour hot sauce on top of batter.
6. Bake in the oven for 40 minutes at 350°F (175°C) or until a toothpick inserted in middle of pudding comes out clean.

SERVES 6

POUDING AU SIROP D'ÉRABLE
Maple Syrup Pudding

1 cup	all purpose flour	250 ml
2 tsp	baking powder	10 ml
1/4 tsp	salt	1 ml
2 tbsp	butter	10 ml
1/4 cup	sugar	60 ml
1	egg	1
1/2 tsp	vanilla	2 ml
2/3 cup	milk	150 ml
1 cup	maple syrup	250 ml
1/4 cup	chopped walnuts (optional)	60 ml

1. Cream butter and sugar. Add egg and mix well.
2. Mix together flour, baking powder and salt. Add this to the batter alternating with milk. Add vanilla.
3. Pour batter in a pan the size of a bread tin and pour maple syrup on top of batter. If nuts are used, sprinkle on top of pudding.
4. Bake at 350°F (175°C) for 45 minutes or until a toothpick inserted in pudding comes out clean.

SERVES 6

Chocolate Pudding

No eggs are used in this recipe. Back in the early days of Quebec, eggs were often scarce in poor families. As an elderly charming lady once told me "We often had to prepare a good nutritious meal with very few ingredients".

1 cup	all purpose flour	250 ml
$^3/_4$ cup	sugar	175 ml
2 tsp	baking powder	10 ml
$^1/_4$ tsp	salt	1 ml
$^1/_3$ cup	cocoa powder	90 ml
2 tbsp	butter	30 ml
$^1/_2$ cup	milk	150 ml
1 tsp	vanilla	5 ml

1. Cream butter and sugar. Add cocoa powder and mix well.
2. Sift flour, baking powder and salt. Blend in this mixture, alternating with milk, to the batter. Add vanilla.
3. Pour batter into a 8 x 8 x 2 inches square pan and set aside while preparing sauce for pudding.

Sauce

2 tbsp	cocoa powder	30 ml
$^1/_2$ cup	brown sugar	125 ml
$^1/_2$ cup	sugar	125 ml
$1^1/_4$ cups	boiling water	280 ml

1. Mix all ingredients and pour on top of pudding batter.

2. Bake at 350°F (175°C) for about 35 minutes or until a toothpick inserted in middle of pudding comes out clean.
3. Serve warm with cream.

SERVES 4 TO 6

POUDING AUX FRAISES
Strawberry Pudding

2 cups	fresh strawberries cut in two	500 ml
¹/₂ cup	brown sugar	125 ml
¹/₂ cup	water	125 ml
Batter		
2 tbsp	butter	30 ml
¹/₂ cup	sugar	125 ml
1	egg, beaten	1
1 cup	all purpose flour	250 ml
1 ¹/₂ tsp	baking powder	7 ml
¹/₄ tsp	salt	1 ml
¹/₃ cup	milk	75 ml

1. Place strawberries in an ovenproof 8 x 8 x 2 inch casserole. Mix brown sugar and water and pour on top of strawberries. Set aside.
2. Cream butter and sugar. Add beaten egg and mix well.
3. Mix flour, baking powder and salt together. Alternately add milk and dry ingredients to mixture.
4. Spoon batter onto top of strawberries and bake at 350°F (175°C) for 30 to 60 minutes until a toothpick inserted in middle of pudding comes out clean.
5. Serve warm with or without cream.

SERVES 4 TO 6

Blueberry Pudding

Berry puddings are prepared in summertime with fresh berries as well as in wintertime with frozen berries. Picking berries is a family affair in Quebec, even young children take part. I always loved picking berries contrary to some of my brothers and sisters who didn't enjoy it as much but had to join anyway. My parents didn't care how many berries we gathered as long as we took part in the work.

This recipe can also be prepared with raspberries. The recipe for batter is the same as used in Poor Man's pudding. The fruit is poured into the baking pan, sprinkled with sugar and topped with batter.

	One recipe of batter (see Poor Man's Pudding)	
4 cups	fresh or frozen blueberries	1 litre
1/2 cup	sugar	125 ml

1. Place blueberries in an ovenproof deep casserole. Sprinkle with sugar.
2. Prepare batter according to recipe in Poor Man Pudding and spoon batter over blueberries.
3. Bake at 350°F (175°C) for about 45 minutes or until a toothpick inserted in the middle of pudding comes out clean.
4. Serve warm with or without cream.

SERVES 4 TO 6

POUDING AUX POMMES
Apple Pudding

This pudding is fast and easy to prepare. Its texture is between that of a cake and a pudding; apple slices are cooked in cake batter. I recommend using tart, juicy apples for this pudding.

5	medium apples, sliced	5
	Brown sugar to cover apple slices	
2 tbsp	soft butter	30 ml
¹/₂ cup	sugar	125 ml
1	egg	1
¹/₂ cup	flour	125 ml
1 tsp	baking powder	5 ml

1. Spread apple slices on the bottom of a greased square pan and sprinkle with brown sugar.
2. In a medium sized bowl, cream butter and sugar. Add egg and mix well.
3. Incorporate flour mixed with baking powder to the batter.
4. Spoon batter onto top of apples and bake at 350°F (175°C) for 45 minutes or until a toothpick inserted in middle of pudding comes out clean.

SERVES 4

CROUSTILLANT AUX POMMES
Apple Crisp

This is one of the first recipes I asked my mother for when I left home. She had learned to prepare it from her mother. It doesn't include spices such as nutmeg or cinnamon in this dessert. Many Quebecers, like my husband, prefer their apple desserts without spices. A good pinch of cinnamon can be added to the flour if you prefer spicy apple desserts.

1 cup	all purpose flour	250 ml
$^1/_2$ cup	brown sugar	125 ml
$^1/_2$ tsp	salt	2 ml
$^1/_4$ cup	softened butter	60 ml
5	apples, sliced	5
	sugar	

1. Place apple slices in the bottom of a greased square pan. Sprinkle apple with sugar.
2. In a medium bowl, mix flour, brown sugar and salt. Mix in butter with fingers or pastry blender. Cover apple with this mixture and bake in a 350°F (175°C) oven for about 30 minutes until crumbly mixture is golden in color.

SERVES 6

CROUSTILLANT À LA RHUBARBE
Rhubarb Crisp

Rhubarb grows well in the cooler Quebec climate. In Quebec most gardeners have their own patch of rhubarb.

4 cups	rhubarb sliced ³/₄ inch (2 cm)	1 litre
1 cup	sugar	250 ml
¹/₄ cup	flour	60 ml
¹/₂ tsp	cinnamon	2 ml
1 cup	flour	250 ml
1 cup	brown sugar	250 ml
¹/₂ cup	oatmeal	125 ml
¹/₂ cup	melted butter	125 ml

1. Mix rhubarb with the cup of sugar, ¹/₄ cup flour and cinnamon. Spread in a 8 x 8 inch pan.
2. In a medium bowl, mix flour, brown sugar and oatmeal. Add melted butter and mix well. Cover rhubarb with this mixture.
3. Cook for 35 minutes at 350°F (175°C).

SERVES 6

GRAND PÈRES AU SIROP D'ÉRABLE

Dumplings in Maple Syrup

1¹/₂ cups	all purpose flour	375 ml
1 tbsp	baking powder	15 ml
¹/₂ tsp	salt	2 ml
3 tbsp	chilled butter	45 ml
¹/₂ cup	milk	125 ml
1¹/₄ cups	preferably dark maple syrup	310 ml
1 cup	water	250 ml
1 cup	heavy cream	250 ml

1. Combine flour, baking powder and salt in a medium bowl. Cut butter into small pieces and scatter over flour mixture. Rub butter and flour between your fingers until mixture resembles coarse meal. Add milk and stir just until batter is uniform. This operation can be done with food processor. Place flour, baking powder and salt into bowl of food processor. Mix a few seconds. Add butter and pulse until it resembles coarse meal. Add milk while it is running and stop machine as soon as a batter forms.
2. In a deep heavy saucepan, bring maple syrup and water to a boil while stirring constantly. Drop tablespoonfuls of batter into boiling syrup, leaving 1 or 2 inch space. Reduce heat to low, cover and simmer for 15 minutes. To check if dumplings are cooked, a toothpick will come out clean when inserted in dumplings.
3. Cool until lukewarm and serve dumplings in a deep bowl ladle with cooking syrup. Serve cream separately in a pitcher. Dumplings are also good without cream if you want to skip the additional calories.

SERVES 6

GRAND PÈRES AUX BLEUETS
Blueberry Dumplings

2 cups	fresh or frozen blueberries	500 ml
1/3 cup	sugar	75 ml
	A pinch of ginger	
1/2 cup	water	125 ml
1 cup	all purpose flour	250 ml
1/4 tsp	salt	1 ml
1/3 cup	milk	75 ml
1/3 cup	brown sugar	75 ml
	A pinch cinnamon	
1 1/2 tsp	baking powder	7 ml
1 tbsp	butter	15 ml

1. In a deep large saucepan, boil blueberries, sugar, ginger and water for 5 minutes.
2. In a medium bowl, mix flour, brown sugar, cinnamon and baking powder. Mix in butter with fingers or pastry blender.
3. Add milk and stir until a uniform batter is formed. To prepare dough in food processor, place flour, brown sugar, cinnamon and baking powder into bowl of food processor. Mix for a few seconds. Add butter and pulse a few times to blend. Add milk while machine is running and stop the motor as soon as dough shapes into a ball around knife.
4. Use a tablespoon to drop batter on top of blueberry sauce, cover and simmer 25 minutes or until a toothpick inserted in dumplings comes out clean.
5. Serve with or without heavy cream.

SERVES 6

GALETTES BLANCHES DE GRAND-MÈRE
Grandmother's White Soft Cookies

Galette in Quebec is a pastry, the size of a large cookie that has a softer texture than a normal cookie and more dense than a cake. Galettes were probably brought to Quebec with the first settlers. The Gazette's Food Editor, Julian Armstrong, told me she had seen similar pastry when she visited the North of France.

I will never forget the taste of these Galettes as prepared by grandma Rose-Anna while my mother was in the hospital giving birth to one of my sisters. With very little in the cupboard, she prepared delicious desserts to last the next few days my mother was going to be away from home.

$^2/_3$ cup	shortening	175 ml
1	egg	1
1 cup	brown sugar	250 ml
1 cup	milk	250 ml
2 tsp	baking powder	10 ml
3 cups	flour	750 ml

1. Cream shortening and sugar. Add egg.
2. Add dry ingredients alternating with milk. Dough will be soft and difficult to manipulate.
3. Generously flour working surface and roll out a third of the dough at a time to a thickness of $^1/_2$ inch (1,5 cm). Generously dust top of dough before rolling out. Cut 3 inch (8 cm) circles of dough, lift carefully with spatula, shake off excess flour by rapidly shifting galette between hands and place on a lightly greased cookie sheet leaving a 2 inch space between galettes.
4. Bake in middle of oven for 15 minutes at 350°F (175°C). Remove galettes from baking sheet with spatula and cool on wire rack. Store in airtight container to prevent drying out and loosing their soft texture.

GALETTES À LA MÉLASSE
Molasses Soft Cookies

1 cup	shortening	250 ml
1 cup	molasses	250 ml
1 cup	brown sugar	250 ml
1 cup	milk	250 ml
1	egg	1
2 tsp	baking soda	10 ml
4 cups	all purpose flour	1 litre
1 tbsp	ground ginger	15 ml

1. Cream shortening. Add brown sugar and egg. Mix well.
2. Dissolve baking soda in molasses and add to the above preparation.
3. Mix flour and ginger , alternately add flour and milk. Stop stirring when batter has a uniform texture.
4. Generously flour working surface, work one third of the dough at a time generously flour top of it before rolling out to a thickness of $1/2$ inch (1,5 cm). With round floured pastry cutter, cut 3 inch (8 cm) "galettes". Lift them carefully with a large spatula and shake off excess flour by rapidly shifting galettes between hands. Place 2 inches (5 cm) apart on a lightly greased cookie sheet.
5. Position oven rack in middle of oven, and bake at 350°F (175°C) for 15 minutes. Remove from cookie sheet with spatula and cool on wire rack. Store in airtight container.

GALETTES AU SIROP
Syrup Soft Cookies

These galettes are a favorite in the Saguenay Lac St-Jean area. Their taste is similar to "Galette à la mélasse" but the texture is slightly different.

$^1/_2$ cup	shortening	125 ml
$^3/_4$ cup	sugar	190 ml
2	eggs	2
$^3/_4$ cup	molasses	190 ml
$^1/_2$ cup	strong coffee	125 ml
$3^1/_4$ cups	all purpose flour	800 ml
$^1/_2$ tsp	salt	2 ml
3 tsp	baking soda	15 ml

1. In a large bowl cream shortening.
2. Add sugar and eggs and beat well. Add molasses.
3. Incorporate coffee.
4. Mix flour, salt and baking soda and add to the batter.
5. Let batter rest for half an hour before rolling out.
6. Roll out dough to a thickness of $^1/_3$ inch (1 cm) on a generously floured surface. Sprinkle top of dough before rolling and cut out 3 inch (8 cm) round pieces with a round pastry cutter.Place 2 inches (5 cm) apart on a lightly greased cookie sheet.
7. Bake for 15 minutes at 375°F (190°C). Cool on wire rack and store in airtight container.

MAKES 2 DOZEN COOKIES

GALETTES AU CHOCOLAT
Chocolate Soft Cookies

1/4 cup	shortening	60 ml
1 cup	brown sugar	250 ml
1	egg	1
1 1/2 cups	all purpose flour	375 ml
1/2 tsp	baking soda	2 ml
1/2 cup	milk	125 ml
2 oz	unsweetened chocolate, melted	60 g
1 cup	chopped nuts (optional)	250 ml
1 tsp	vanilla	5 ml

1. Cream shortening. Add brown sugar and beat in egg.
2. Mix flour with baking soda and alternately add it and the milk to the batter.
3. Add melted chocolate and vanilla and chopped nuts.
4. Drop heaped tablespoonfuls of batter onto a lightly greased and floured cookie sheet and bake in middle of oven at 350°F (175°C) for 15 minutes.
5. Cool on wire rack and store in airtight container.

GALETTES À LA CITROUILLE

Pumpkin Soft Cookies

These "galettes" can be prepared with canned or frozen pureed pumpkin. They can be eaten freshly baked but the flavor improves after a day.

1¼ cups	all purpose flour	310 ml
²/₃ cup	brown sugar	175 ml
1	egg, beaten	1
¼ cup	soft butter	60 ml
³/₄ cup	pumpkin pureed	190 ml
1½ tsp	baking powder	7 ml
½ tsp	cinnamon	2 ml
1¼ tsp	ground nutmeg	6 ml
⅛ tsp	ground ginger	0,5 ml
¼ cup	raisin	60 ml
½ cup	chopped nuts	125 ml

1. Cream butter, add brown sugar.
2. Add beaten egg and mix well. Mix in pureed pumpkin.
3. Mix flour with baking powder, cinnamon, nutmeg and ginger. Add to the first preparation. Add raisins and chopped nuts.
4. Drop heaping tablespoonfuls of batter, two inches apart, onto an ungreased cookie sheet. Position oven rack in middle of oven and bake cookies for 15 minutes at 400°F (220°C).

Batter can be mixed in a food processor. Do not overbeat.

GALETTES AUX BLEUETS
Blueberry Soft Cookies

¹/₄ cup	shortening	60 ml
¹/₄ cup	soft butter	60 ml
1 cup	brown sugar	250 ml
3	eggs, beaten	3
²/₃ cup	milk	175 ml
1³/₄ cups	all purpose flour	440 ml
2 tsp	baking powder	10 ml
1 tsp	baking soda	5 ml
¹/₂ tsp	salt	2 ml
1 tsp	vanilla	5 ml
1 cup	fresh or frozen blueberries	250 ml

1. Cream together butter and shortening and add brown sugar.
2. Add beaten eggs and milk.
3. Mix flour, baking powder, baking soda and salt and add to batter. Add vanilla and fold in blueberries.
4. Drop by tablespoon onto greased cookie sheet and cook in middle of oven for 15 minutes at 350°F (175°C).

Doughnuts

Doughnuts are very popular around Christmas time. They are prepared one or two weeks before Christmas and frozen. My grandmother taught me that their taste improve when frozen. She baked the best doughnuts I have ever tasted. These were served at New Year's dinner, which was the biggest gathering of the year. We were about forty people in a small city apartment. She knew how fond I was of her doughnuts, so she would wrap a few in a paper napkin and hide them in her clothes drawer. At the end of the evening, I would secretly recover my "treasure" without anyone noticing. Years ago,before freezers were invented, doughnuts were kept outside in a small roomcalled "cuisine d'été " attached to the house or apartment. Make sure you use a deep casserole to prevent danger of fire while frying.

$^1/_2$ cup	butter (room temperature)	125 ml
$2^1/_2$ cups	brown sugar	625 ml
7	eggs	7
$1^1/_2$ cups	milk	375 ml
$7^1/_2$ cups	all purpose flour	1,75 litres
3 tsp	baking powder	15 ml

1. Mix together butter, brown sugar and eggs. Alternately add flour mixed with baking powder and milk. Mix until batter is smooth.
2. Generously flour working surface and place a third of dough on flour. Generously sprinkle dough with flour and roll to a thickness of $^3/_4$ inch (2 cm) and cut with floured doughnut cutter. Place doughnut on a lightly floured surface before frying.
3. Heat, in at least 4 inches (10 cm) deep of vegetable oil at 365°F (185°C) and fry 3 or 4 doughnuts at a time for about 2 minutes on each side or until golden. Remove doughnuts

with slotted spoon and drain on brown paper.
4. If eaten fresh, coat doughnuts with icing sugar by dipping in a bowl of icing sugar. If frozen, defrost doughnuts in a warm oven and coat with icing sugar as directed above.

TARTE AU SUCRE
Sugar Pie

This is the most popular dessert in Quebec Cuisine. It's very sweet. I think the comment from a teenager male guest from Toronto describes well "Tarte au sucre". When I asked him if he liked it after a second helping he said: "It's very sweet but It's so good". Be sure to accompany "Tarte au sucre" with a glass of cold milk to counteract the sweet taste.

There are so many versions of it that it seems every family has its own recipe. I have four versions in my file but the following has been the favorite in my family. For best results, use pale brown sugar.

$^3/_4$ cup	pale brown sugar	190 ml
3 tbsp	milk or cream	45 ml
1 tbsp	butter cut in dices	15 ml
1	pie shell, unbaked	1

1. In a small bowl, mix together, brown sugar and milk or cream. Pour mixture into pie shell and scatter diced butter on top of it.
2. Bake pie for 20 to 25 minutes at 400°F (220°C) or until pie dough is golden.

SERVES 6

TARTE À LA MÉLASSE
Molasses Pie

This is a favorite in my husband's family.

¹/₂ cup	molasses	125 ml
1 tbsp	all purpose flour	15 ml
1 tbsp	vinegar	15 ml
1 tbsp	water	15 ml
1	pie shell, unbaked	1

1. In a small bowl, blend molasses with flour. Add water and vinegar.
2. Pour this preparation into an unbaked pie shell and bake for 20 minutes at 400°F (220°C).

SERVES 6

TARTE AUX POMMES
Apple Pie

Apple is a popular fruit in Quebec. There are many orchards in the southern parts of the province. In early autumn, on weekends, many like to combine a short nature trip in nature to see the beautiful colors of tree leaves and to pick fresh apples in orchards. I still remember when I lived in Hawkesbury, Ontario, on the Quebec border, I would pick up my dear friend Francine early in the morning for a "food trip". Our first stop was at the market in Lachute where we would buy fresh vegetables from the farmers area. The second stop was at the Oka monastery to buy fresh rounds of the famous Oka cheese and from there, we would go on to St-Joseph du Lac to gather MacIntosh apples. Simple things in life often bring you great joy!

¹/₂ cup	sugar	125 ml
3 tbsp	all purpose flour	45 ml
	A pinch of salt	
5 cups	thinly sliced peeled "MacIntosh" apples or other tart apples	1,25 litres
1 tbsp	butter	15 ml
2	unbaked pie crusts	2

1. Heat oven at 425°F (220°C). Cover bottom of pie plate with one crust.
2. Mix sugar, flour and salt in a medium bowl. Add sliced apples and stir gently to coat with flour mixture; pour into pie plate. Scatter butter cut in dices over apple mixture. Spread a mixture of egg beaten with a little bit of milk on pie border, place second crust on top of apples and press gently to seal pie. Brush pie with egg mixture except border and cut a few slits to help steam escape.
3. Bake for 15 minutes, lower oven temperature to 375° (190°C) and bake for another 25 minutes. Cool before serving.

SERVES 6

TARTE AUX BLEUETS
Blueberry Pie

The blueberry is the official symbol of the Saguenay-Lac- St-Jean area. Blueberries are so prolific in that region that there are many "U-pick" farms as well as industries that freeze blueberries to ship away and transform them into products such as alcoholic beverages, jams etc... People of the Saguenay-Lac-St-Jean area like to tease other Quebecers by telling them that their blueberries are so big in their area that it takes only three of them to bake a pie.

2	unbaked pie crusts	2
3 cups	fresh blueberries	750 ml
4 tbsp	all purpose flour	60 ml
²/₃ cup	sugar	150 ml
2 tbsp	butter	30 ml

1. Heat oven to 425°F (220°C).In a medium bowl, mix flour and sugar.
2. Transfer blueberries and stir to coat them with sugar mixture.
3. Turn blueberries into pastry lined pie pan. Dot with butter.
4. Brush border of pie with an egg beaten with a little bit of milk, cover blueberries with top crust pressing gently to seal pie.
5. Trim and flute border, brush center of pie with egg mixture and cut a few slits. Bake for 15 minutes, lower oven temperature to 350°F (175°C) and bake for another 20 to 30 minutes until crust is light brown. Cool before serving.

SERVES 6

TARTE AUX RAISINS DE MAMAN
Mom's Raisin Pie

I have tasted many raisin pies but I still think my mother has the secret for the best one.

2	unbaked pie crusts	2
2 cups	cold water	500 ml
2 cups	Sultana raisins	500 ml
¹/₂ cup	brown sugar	125 ml
2 tbsp	all purpose flour	30 ml
1 tbsp	butter	15 ml

1. Heat oven to 425°F (220°C).
2. Place water and raisins in a medium saucepan, bring to boil and cook on medium heat for 5 minutes.
3. Mix flour and brown sugar, add to raisins with constant stirring and cook for about 1 minutes until mixture thickens. Incorporate butter and cool completely before using. This can be done a few hours in advance.
4. Pour raisins in pastry-lined pie pan, brush border with beaten egg mixed with a little bit of milk, cover with top crust and press gently to seal crusts. Cut and flute border, brush pie with egg mixture except border and cut a few slits in top crust.
5. Bake for 15 minutes, lower oven temperature to 375°F (190°C) and bake for another 20 to 30 minutes until crust is light brown. Cool before serving.

SERVES 6

CIPÂTE AUX BLEUETS
Deep Dish Blueberry Pie

This dessert is a Lac St-Jean speciality. Instead of having the pie pan lined with pie crust, the crust is placed in the center of the blueberries. The berry juice permeates the crust which gives this pie its special taste and texture. This method is also used to prepare a meat pie containing different kinds of meat and potatoes.

2	unbaked pie crusts	2
5 cups	blueberries	1,25 litres
1¹/₄ cups	sugar	310 ml
2 tbsp	butter	30 ml

1. Heat oven to 350°F (175°C). Pour half of blueberries into a deep dish casserole. Sprinkle with half of sugar and cover with a pie crust; trim crust to fit into dish.
2. Cover crust with other half of blueberries, sprinkle with remaining sugar and dot with butter. Cover with top crust and trim edge to fit border of casserole. Cut a 2 inch (5 cm) hole in center of pie; this will allow steam to escape.
3. Bake for about two hours or until crust is light brown. Cool until lukewarm and serve with pouring cream if desired.

SERVES **6**

Blueberry Pudding (p.110)

Sugarhouse

Sleigh Ride heading to the sugarhouse

COMPOTE DE POMMES
Apple Sauce

8	apples peeled and thinly sliced	8
1 cup	water	250 ml
	A pinch of salt	
1/2 cup	sugar	125 ml

1. Put all ingredients in a large saucepan, bring to a boil and cook on medium heat for 20 minutes with occasional stirring. Cool completely before serving.

SERVES 4 TO 6

MOUSSE AUX POMMES

Apple Mousse

This is a last minute dessert that should be eaten no later than one hour after it has been prepared.

8	apples	8
3 tbsp	brown sugar	45 ml
2 tbsp	water	30 ml
1 tsp	cinnamon	5 ml
3	egg whites	3
3 tbsp	brown sugar	45 ml

1. Peel and thinly slice apples. Place in a medium saucepan, add water plus 3 tbsp brown sugar. Cook uncovered on medium heat until apples transform into a purée.
2. Pass through a strainer to get a fine purée or use a food processor to do the job.
3. Beat egg whites with a pinch of salt until they begin to hold their own shape. Gradually add sugar and continue to beat until stiff.
4. With a spatula, gently fold apple purée into the egg white mixture and then pour into four small dessert cups.

SERVES 4

130

TARTINE À L'ÉRABLE
Maple Sugar Treat

This dessert is as delicious as it is simple to prepare. Use homemade or thick slices of bread if possible.

For one portion, spread one slice of white bread with grated maple sugar and cover with a thin layer of light or heavy cream.

PÂTE À TARTE
Pie Dough

2²/₃ cups	all purpose flour	675 ml
1 tsp	salt	5 ml
1 cup	vegetable shortening or pure lard	250 ml
1 cup	cold water (approximatively)	250 ml

1- Mix salt and flour in a large bowl. Scatter vegetable shortening in six pieces over flour mixture. Combine with fat with a pastry blender until mixture is crumbly and has bits pieces the size of a pea.

2- Sprinkle cold water over mixture and blend by passing a fork through the mixture until it begins to form a ball. Add more water, a few tbsp at a time, if needed to bind in a ball. Finish working dough with your hands but do not over-manipulate, otherwise dough will be though.

3- Wrap dough in wax paper and let stand a few minutes before using. At this point, dough can be refrigerated for 3 days or frozen but should be brought up at room temperature before using.

4- On a floured board, roll pieces of dough to a thickness of ¹/₄ inch (0,5 cm) turning flipping at least once during this operation; this will prevent dough from sticking to the board. For a double crust pie, seal crusts with a mixture of one egg beaten with a little milk and brush top crust with the same mixture, except edge of pie. Slit top crust a few times before baking. For a baked shell, prick shell and place a light pie plate or a few light aluminum pie plates for the first 15 minutes of baking and remove pie plate to finish baking; pie plate will easily be removed when it's time to take it off. Cook for another 10 to15 minutes until pie shell is light brown.

3 CRUSTS

CANDIES

SUCRE À LA CRÈME
Penuche

Penuche was our Sunday afternoon family gathering treat. Grandmother would prepare a batch of the sweet squares while everybody chatted about the latest news in or outside the family.

1 cup	sugar	250 ml
1 cup	brown sugar	250 ml
1 cup	heavy cream	250 ml
1 tbsp	butter	15 ml
$^1/_2$ tsp	vanilla	3 ml
$^1/_2$ cup	chopped walnuts (if desired)	125 ml

1. Mix sugar, brown sugar. Gradually add cream.
2. Bring to a boil on medium heat stirring constantly. Cook on medium heat without stirring until a candy thermometer registers 240°F (116°C).
3. Remove from heat, cool for half an hour, add butter and vanilla and beat until mixture loses its shiny look.Mix in walnuts, pour in a buttered 8 x 8 inch (20 x 20 cm) square pan, cool to room temperature and cut in one inch (2,5 cm) squares. Keep in a container with a tight fitting cover.

TIRE STE-CATHERINE
St.Catherine Taffy

This treat was prepared to be served on November 25th. That day was designed to honour young ladies over the age of 25, who were still unmarried (old maids). To pull taffy, generously butter hands, pull taffy two feet long, fold in two and pull again until taffy is of desired color.

1 cup	sugar	250 ml
1 cup	brown sugar	250 ml
1/2 cup	dark corn syrup	125 ml
1 tbsp	vinegar	15 ml
1 cup	molasses	250 ml
1 tsp	butter	5 ml
1 tsp	baking soda	5 ml

1. Place all ingredients except the baking soda in a medium saucepan. Cook and stir on medium heat until boiling.
2. Cook on medium heat without stirring until temperature reaches 264°F (129°C) on a candy thermometer.
3. Remove from heat, add sifted baking soda and mix well.
4. Pour into 3 or 4 greased pie plates, cool until lukewarm and pull until taffy becomes beige color. Stretch in a long rope one inch (2,5 cm) thick and cut in one inch (2,5 cm) lengths. Wrap each candy in wax paper.

TIRE ÉPONGE

Sponge Taffy

Children love the crunchie texture of this candy. When I was young we could buy a fairly big piece for only a nickel.

1 cup	sugar	250 ml
1 cup	corn syrup	250 ml
4 tsp	baking soda	20 ml

1. Heat sugar and corn syrup in a medium saucepan until a spoonful of the mixture, dropped into a glass of very cold water, forms a hard thread.
2. Add baking soda, mix well and pour on a cookie sheet. Cool and break into pieces.

PRESERVES

Since Quebec has a short summer season that provides fresh vegetables for such a short period, preserving is very popular. Even though a good part of fresh fruits and vegetables are frozen, tradition is still strong when it comes to pickling and jam making.

The smell of ketchup or jam simmering on the stove is as rewarding as the taste of homemade preserves. What a gift idea !

KETCHUP AUX TOMATES ROUGES
Red Tomato ketchup

Ketchup is usually served with meat pie or roast meat such as veal or pork.

24	fresh tomatoes	24
6	apples	6
6	large onions	6
1	head of celery	1
1/4 cup	pickling spices	60 ml
2 tsp	salt	10 ml
1/2 tsp	ground clove	2 ml
1/2 tsp	ground ginger	2 ml
2 cups	white vinegar	500 ml
2 1/2 cups	brown sugar	625 ml

1. Blanch tomatoes in boiling water until skin starts to crack open. Place in cold water for a few minutes, peel and cut into big pieces.
2. Peel apples and cut into cubes.
3. Peel and thinly slice onions.
4. Wash and chop celery. Wrap pickling spices in a piece of cheese cloth.
5. Place all ingredients, except brown sugar, in a large kettle. Bring to a boil and simmer for 1 hour.
6. Add brown sugar and cook for another hour, stirring often, until ketchup thickens.
7. Remove bag of pickling spices and then pour the mixture into sterilized jars sealing with new mason jar lids.

KETCHUP AUX TOMATES VERTES
Green Tomato Ketchup

24	green tomatoes	24
15	onions	15
1	head of celery	1
4 cups	white vinegar	1 litre
6 cups	white sugar	1,5 litres
$^1/_2$ cup	pickling spices	125 ml
6 tbsp	coarse salt	90 ml
1 tsp	cinnamon	5 ml

1. Wash, remove stem end and core and cut tomatoes in pieces.
2. Peel and slice onions. Wrap pickling spices in cheesecloth.
3. Chop celery.
4. Place all ingredients in a large kettle and cook for 2 to 3 hours until slightly thickened.
5. Pour in hot sterilized jars and close with new lids.

BETTERAVES MARINÉES
Pickled Beets

My mother has a very simple way to prepare pickled beets. She pours a mixture of half water half vinegar over cooked, peeled beets. Thats the way I prefer them but if you like spicy, marinated ones, the following recipe is as delicious.

4 lb	beets, cooked and peeled	2 kg
2¹/₂ cups	vinegar	625 ml
¹/₂ cup	water	125 ml
1¹/₄ cups	sugar	310 ml
1 tbsp	pickling salt	15 ml
3	medium onions, sliced	3
6	whole cloves	6
	A pinch of ground cinnamon	

1. In a non reactive pan, bring water, vinegar, sugar and salt to boil.
2. Add beets, onions and spices. Simmer a few minutes and pour into hot sterilized jars. Seal.

RELISH AUX CONCOMBRES
Cucumber Relish

I suggest using very large cucumbers for this recipe. This relish is very good with hot dogs.

6 cups	ground unpeeled cucumbers	1,5 litres
1 cup	onion, chopped very finely	250 ml
2 tbsp	sweet red pepper, chopped very finely	30 ml
1 tbsp	pickling salt	15 ml
1¼ cups	vinegar	310 ml
¾ cup	white sugar	175 ml
½ tsp	salt	2 ml

1. Cut cucumbers lengthwise, remove seeds with a spoon and pass through a grinder.
2. Add onions, red pepper and salt. Let stand for one hour. Strain mixture.
3. In a saucepan, bring to boil, vinegar and sugar. Add drained vegetables, pour into hot sterilized jar and seal.

MAKES 3 PINTS

Winter Salad

7 lb	red tomatoes	3 kg
1	head celery	1
1	green pepper	1
6	large onions	6
¹/₂ cup	pickling salt	125 ml
3 cups	sugar	750 ml
2 cups	vinegar	500 ml
¹/₄ cup	mustard seed	60 ml

1. Chop vegetables in fairly small pieces.
2. Add pickling salt, mix well and let soak overnight.
3. Drain well, add sugar, vinegar and mustard seed. Let stand for 12 hours stirring often.
4. Pack into sterilized jars and seal. Store in a cold storage or preferably in a refrigerator.

Salted Herbs

Salted herbs are frequently used in traditional Quebec cuisine. In early times, this was the only way to preserve fresh herbs to season soup, ragout, etc... in the winter months. You can leave out one herb and add more of another as long as you have the same amount of salt for the total amount of fresh herbs.

1 cup	fresh chives, chopped finely	250 ml
1 cup	fresh parsley, chopped finely	250 ml
1 cup	leeks, chopped finely	250 ml
1 cup	green parts of scallion, chopped finely	250 ml
2 cups	celery leaves, chopped finely	500 ml
1/2 cup	fresh savory, chopped finely	125 ml
1/4 cup	fresh sage, chopped finely	60 ml
2 cups	pickling salt	500 ml

1. Herbs should be washed and dried first. Chop them before measuring.
2. Mix chopped herbs in a large bowl.
3. In glass jars, alternate layers of salt and fresh herbs finishing with salt. Close top and store in refrigerator. Salted herbs will keep well for one year.
4. To season soups and stew, scoop a large spoonful from the jar and rinse under cold water to remove excess salt before using.

MAKES 4 PINTS

CONFITURE DE FRAMBOISES
Raspberry Jam

Raspberries grow wild in every part of Quebec. It is possible to pick raspberries at U-pick farms but many people still prefer picking wild raspberries because they have more flavor than the ones grown on the farms.

8 cups	fresh or frozen raspberries without syrup	2 litres
6 cups	white sugar	1,5 litres
2 cups	water	500 ml
1	pouch of liquid pectin	1

1. In a large kettle, boil water and sugar until a teaspoon of syrup, dropped into cold water, forms a thread.
2. Add raspberries and boil for 10 minutes.
3. Add pectin and continue cooking for 1 minute while constantly stirring.
4. Pour jam into hot sterilized jars. Close jars and cool completely before storing.

To sterilize jars, place in a 250°F (120°C) oven for 30 minutes. If using mason jars, boil new lids for one minute and use them to seal jars while jam is still hot. This way you don't have to use wax to seal jars.

MAKES 4 PINTS

CONFITURE DE FRAISES
Strawberry Jam

8 cups	fresh strawberries	2 litres
8 cups	sugar	2 litres
1	pouch of liquid pectin	1

1. Wash strawberries only if soil is clinging to the fruit. Remove stalks.
2. In a large kettle, alternate layers of strawberries and sugar, finishing with sugar. Let sit overnight.
3. Cook on low heat until sugar is melted. On medium heat, continue cooking for $1/2$ hour skimming when necessary.
4. Add pectin and cook for one minute stirring constantly.
5. Pour in hot sterilized jars and seal (see note on raspberry jam).

MAKES 4 PINTS

MENUS

Sugar Party

With the first warm sunny days of early spring, usually in March, the sugar farmer starts to collect maple sap and transform it into maple syrup, maple butter, maple sugar and maple taffy. The latter is especially good when poured from the kettle on fresh clean snow while still hot. Quebec is the world's leading producer of maple products. Most of it comes from the Beauce area.

As soon as the sugar maker has enough maple products to feed many people, sugar parties are organized for family and friends. Everybody meets at the sap house where the maple sap is taken to be boiled down from which all of the delicious maple products are obtained. Many give a helping hand to gather the maple sap and everyone shares a meal of dishes that have been prepared with plenty of maple syrup poured on top. The best part of the meal is the dessert which consist of hot maple taffy poured onto fresh snow. Guests are invited to go outside, where they are given a spatula to roll the taffy while it is still warm.

After the meal, tables are put aside and the party goes on with singing and dancing until the end of the evening.

The following menu is usually served at sugar parties:

CABANE À SUCRE - **Sugar Party**

Baked Beans

Boiled potatoes

Boiled ham

Grilled slices of salted pork

Poached Eggs in syrup

Pancakes

Bread

Husking bee

Epluchette is a corn-husking party. In the early days of Quebec, young ladies and men met at the husk to peel corn. Today's corn-husking parties are still held and guests don't have to husk corn anymore. Fresh picked corn is boiled in a large kettle in the backyard.

Christmas in Quebec

Christmas is the most important celebration of the year in Quebec. Families gather after the midnight mass to exchange wishes and share food for the Merry Season. The party goes on often until the early morning hours. This custom was brought from France by early settlers; it's called "Le Réveillon" which means "Christmas Eve party".

On Christmas Eve, children go to bed early and must stay quiet, even though they're anxious to see what they'll get as Christmas gift. They are told that "Santa Claus will visit while they're sleeping".

Around midnight, children are awakened and invited to the Christmas tree to unwrap their gift "brought by Santa Claus". The party goes on, with everybody chatting, singing or dancing until the middle of the night. Then the table is set and a "Réveillon" menu is served buffet style. On Christmas day, the festivities go on with a Christmas dinner usually being served in another relative's home. The traditional dessert for the occasion (which also dates back to France) is the Yule Log, a white jelly roll cake iced with chocolate buttercream.

Following are examples of a "Réveillon" and a Christmas dinner menu.

RÉVEILLON - **Christmas Eve**

Fancy chicken , ham and egg sandwiches

"Tourtière" or "paté à la viande"

Pickle, green ketchup and stuffed olives

Galettes, Doughnuts and fancy cookies

SOUPER DE NOËL - **Christmas Dinner**

Roast beef or Roast Turkey

Mashed potatoes

Buttered carrots

Pickled beets

Green salad

Yule Log served with ice cream

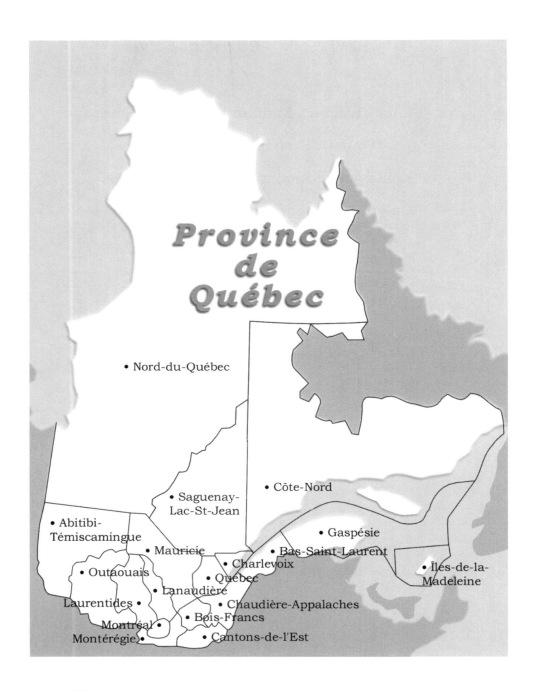

Province
de
Québec

• Nord-du-Québec

• Côte-Nord

• Saguenay-
Lac-St-Jean

• Abitibi-
Témiscamingue

• Gaspésie

• Mauricie

• Bas-Saint-Laurent

• Outaouais

• Charlevoix

• Québec

• Îles-de-la-
Madeleine

• Lanaudière

Laurentides •

• Chaudière-Appalaches

Montréal •

• Bois-Francs

Montérégie •

• Cantons-de-l'Est

INDEX

Apple
    Apple Crisp 112
    Apple Mousse 130
    Apple Pie 124
    Apple Pudding 111
    Apple Sauce 129

Beans
    Baked Beans and Pork 38
    Beans and Partridges 85
    Broad Beans Soup 23
    Maple Syrup Baked Beans 39
    Marinated Broad Beans 18

Beef
    Beef Roll 72
    Boiled Beef and Vegetables 68
    Deep Dish Meat Pie 58
    Homemade Sausages 53
    Mummy's Tomato Meatloaf 70
    Quebec Sheperd's Pie 71

Beet
    Pickled Beets 140

Blood Pudding
    Blood Pudding in White Sauce 63

Blueberry
    Blueberry Dumplings 115
    Blueberry Pie 126
    Blueberry Soft Cookies 121
    Deep Dish Blueberry Pie 128

Bread
    French Toasts 34

Cabbage
    Cabbage Soup 22
    Partridge with Cabbage 86
    Sauteed Cabbage and Onions 94

Cake
    Butter Cake 96
    Buttercake with Penuche Sauce 97
    Caramel Cake 98
    Small Chocolate Cream Filled Cakes 104
    Yule Log 102

Candy
    Penuche 134
    Sponge Taffy 136
    St.Catherine Taffy 135

Carrot
    Mashed Potatoes and Carrots 93

Cereal
    Buckwheat Pancakes 36
    Oatmeal Porridge 37
    Pancakes 35

Cookie
    Blueberry Soft Cookies 121
    Chocolate Soft Cookies 119
    Grandmother's White Soft Cookies 116
    Molasses Soft Cookies 117
    Pumpkin Soft Cookies 120
    Syrup Soft Cookies 118

Cucumber
    Cucumber Relish 141

Doughnuts
    Doughnuts 122

Dumplings
    Blueberry Dumplings 115
    Dumplings in Maple Syrup 114

Egg
    Eggs in a White Onion Sauce 90
    Pickled Eggs 91
    Salted Pork Omelette 89

Fish

Cod in Tomato Soup 43
Fish and Chips 49
Fish Chowder 41
Fried Smelts 42
Iles de Sorel Fricassee 48
Landlocked Salmon Tourtière 45
Oven Baked Landlocked Salmon 44
Potato Salmon Pie 46
Salmon Sauce 47

Game
Beans and Partridges 85
Braised Pheasant 87
Cognac Flambé Partridge 84
Creamed Partridge 83
Deep Dish Meat Pie 58
Moose Roast 82
Partridge with Cabbage 86

Jam
Raspberry Jam 144
Strawberry Jam 145

ketchup
Green Tomato Ketchup 139
Red Tomato ketchup 138

Leftover beef
Quebec Sheperd's Pie 71

Maple
Dumplings in Maple Syrup 114
Maple Pork Chops 56
Maple Sugar Treat 131
Maple Syrup Baked Beans 39
Maple Syrup Pudding 107

Onion
Eggs in a White Onion Sauce 90
Sauteed Cabbage and Onions 94

Pancake
Buckwheat Pancakes 36

Pancakes   35

Partridge
    Beans and Partridges 85
    Cognac Flambé Partridge 84
    Cream of Partridge Soup 30
    Creamed Partridge 83
    Partridge with Cabbage 86

Pickle
    Cucumber Relish 141
    Green Tomato Ketchup 139
    Pickled Beets 140
    Red Tomato ketchup 138
    Winter Salad 142

Pie
    Apple Pie 124
    Blueberry Pie 126
    Deep Dish Blueberry Pie 128
    Deep Dish Meat Pie 58
    Meatpie 60
    Molasses Pie 124
    Mom's Raisin Pie 127
    Pie dough 132
    Potato Salmon Pie 46
    Quebec Sheperd's Pie 71
    Saguenay Meat and Game Pie 87
    Sugar Pie 123

Pork
    Baked Beans and Pork 38
    Blood Pudding in White Sauce 63
    Deep Dish Meat Pie 58
    Grilled Slices of Salted Pork 19
    Homemade Sausages 53
    Maple Pork Chops 56
    Meatpie 60
    Microwaved Potted Pork 17
    Pig's Feet and Meatball Ragout 54
    Pork Roast and Yellow Potatoes 51
    Potted Pork 16

Roast Dripping Jelly 20
Roast Pork and Roast Dripping Jelly 52
Salted Pork 64
Salted Pork Omelette 89

Potato
    Mashed Potatoes and Carrots 93
    Pork Roast and Yellow Potatoes 51
    Potato Salmon Pie 46
    Roast Potatoes 94

Poultry
    Chicken au Gratin 80
    Roast Chicken and Meatballs 78

Pudding
    Apple Pudding 111
    Chocolate Pudding 108
    Maple Syrup Pudding 107
    Poor Man's Pudding 106
    Strawberry Pudding 109

Pumpkin
    Pumpkin Soft Cookies 120

Relish
    Cucumber Relish 141

Rhubarb
    Rhubarb Crisp 113

Salted Herbs
    Salted Herbs 143

Sausages
    Homemade Sausages 53

Soup
    Broad Beans Soup 23
    Cabbage Soup 22
    Cod in Tomato Soup 43
    Cream of Partridge Soup 30
    Drunkard Soup 24
    Fish Chowder 41

Hominy and Vegetable Soup 29
Pea Soup 25
Tomato and Milk Soup 26
Vegetable and Meatball Soup 28
Vegetable Soup 27

Strawberry
Strawberry Jam 145
Strawberry Pudding 109

Tomato
Cod in Tomato Soup 43
Green Tomato Ketchup 139
Mummy's Tomato Meatloaf 70
Red Tomato ketchup 138
Tomato and Milk Soup 26

Veal
Deep Dish Meat Pie 58

Vegetable
Boiled Beef and Vegetables 68
Mashed Potatoes and Carrots 93
Roast Potatoes 94
Sauteed Cabbage and Onions 94

Order Form

I would like to receive:

N. of copies

Traditional Quebec Cooking, ...16.95$_____

Eastern Townships Traditional Cooking, 14.95$_____

A Taste of Maple, ...16.95$_____

Add 5.00$ for shipping cost
Canadian residents, add 7% GST
U.S. residents pay in U.S. funds

Amount included: . . . . ._____$

Please send check or money order to:

Les Editions La Bonne Recette
460 St-Antoine
St-Irénée, QC
Canada, G0T 1V0
www3.sympatico.ca/edition.bonnerecette

Name: . . . .

Address: . . . .

City: . . . .

Prov./State: . . . .

Country: . . . . .Postal Code/Zip: . . . .